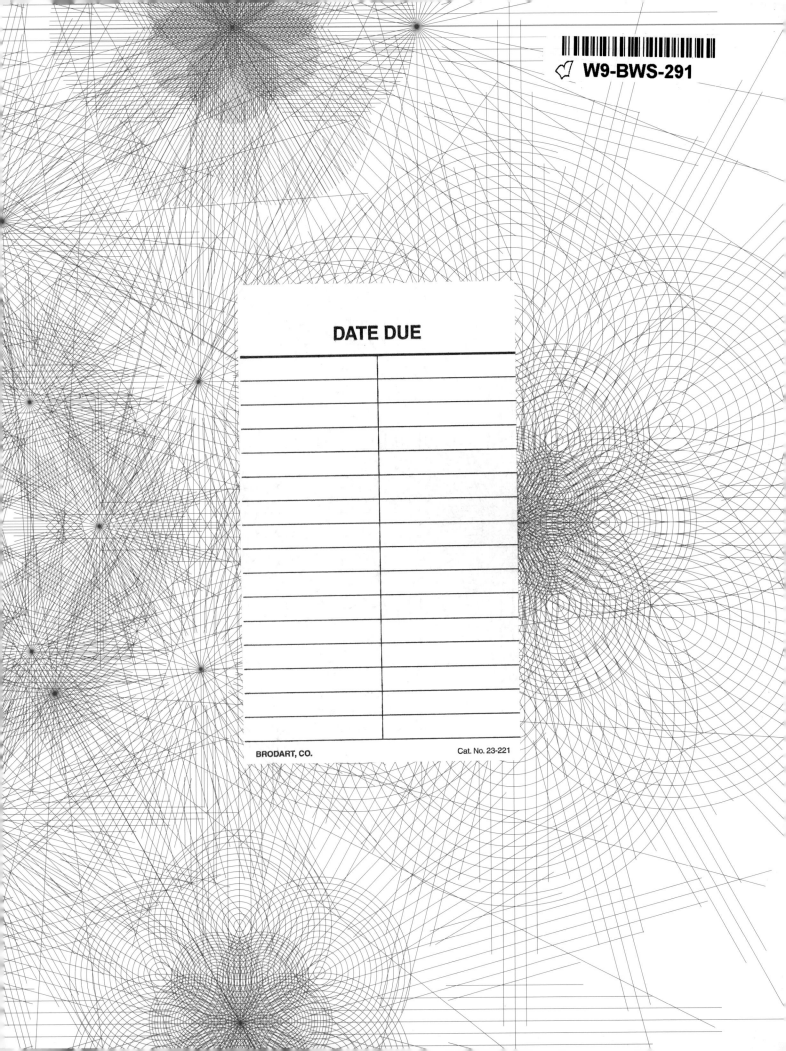

THE BEST OF

BROCHURE DESIGN 12

748 plates and
details of
140 brochures from
65 firms in
16 countries

Public

First published in the United States of America by Rockport Publishers, a member of Quayside Publishing Group

100 Cummings Center
Suite 406-L
Beverly, Massachusetts 01915-6101
Telephone: (978) 282-9590
Fax: (978) 283-2742
www.rockpub.com

**Library of Congress
Cataloging-in-Publication available**

ISBN: 978-1-59253-833-1

Digital edition published in 2013
eISBN-13: 978-1-61058-782-2

10 9 8 7 6 5 4 3 2

Design: Public, San Francisco
publicdesign.com

Printed in China

Contents

Introduction

We've all heard the "end of print" declaration for years. Lately, it seems as if we're running a horse-and-buggy company hoping that the automobile won't catch on. Nowhere has this been more apparent than in the world of the print brochure. Once a mainstay of our business, nowadays they are the rarity. Etc, etc, etc . . .

But wait. Along comes Rockport Publishers with its Best of Brochure Design series and, "Boom!" we're transported into a world where a fascination for the analog is still at full throttle. In an almost nostalgic state, we experience the simple joy of turning pages, unfolding, scale, ink, and paper, of texture, and of physical presence. There is something so wonderfully human about the printed brochure. It demands our interaction. You can touch it, pick it up—it has weight—even smell the ink. You sense the artful hand, the care and craft. It sits there on your table, not moving, and when you come back the next day, it's still there.

A well-executed brochure allows multiple facets of a company's personality to shine. The format forms and informs the narrative. The pacing and rhythm shape the experience. Brochures feature and showcase not only design and brand but photographers, illustrators, writers, fonts, materials, texture, and color— and the art and craft of printing.

We should really have called this book *The Best of Brochure Design Sent to Public.* The more brochures that came through our doors, the better they got. We began to wonder how many more examples of envious talent and beauty were out there that had not made their way to us.

In our studio, at this moment, are boxes filled with well-planned, artfully executed, and thoroughly creative objects from around the world. The process of reviewing this work has left us feeling slightly awkward for judging it, lucky for the opportunity, and truly inspired and energized by the experience.

Todd, Tessa, Nancy, Lindsay, Nick, Dave

Public

Thank you to all the designers who submitted work for this book.
And our utmost appreciation and enduring admiration to
Julia, Martin, Guto, and Dave for sharing their work and
thoughts on brochures and brochure design.

Unending gratitude to Jonathan and Winnie for shooting
the brochures with us—your talents far exceeded our needs,
but the results far exceeded our expectations.

This book is dedicated to Ellis, Smith, Nova, Orin, Gianni, Stella,
and Katrina who hold the future of everything.

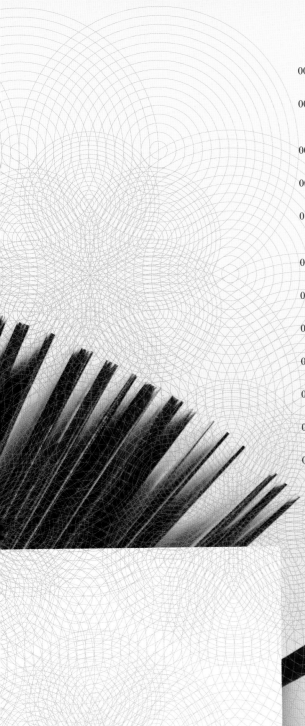

small

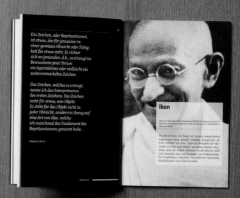

Title: Semiotik Booklet
Firm: 804© Agentur für visuelle Kommunikation
Art Directors: Oliver Henn, Helge Rieder, Carsten Prenger
Designers: Carsten Prenger, Sebastian Hähnlein
Client: 804©

Printer: Alphaprint, Duesseldorf
Method: 4 color

Fonts: Skolar, Taz III

Designer's Statement:

The 804© thematic booklets cope with different areas of communication design short and to the point. Theory and methodology of each topic are complemented by examples, anecdotes, and case studies from everyday practice.

This makes the booklets interesting for such clients who would like to get an easy introduction to the complex topics. Thematic booklets about the naming process, semiotics, and wayfinding have already been published in this series.

The *Naming Booklet* enables the reader to dive into the subject matter of name finding.

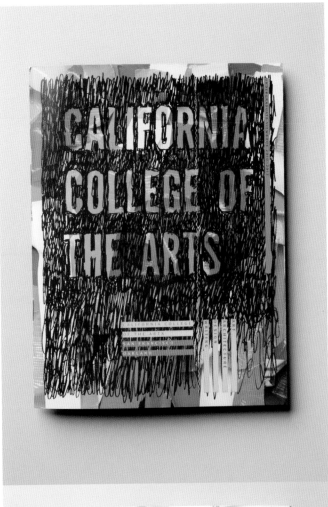

Title: CCA Undergraduate Viewbook
2011–2012
Firm: Aufuldish & Warinner
Designer: Bob Aufuldish
Client: California College of the Arts
Client Industry: Education/Academia

Printer: American Web
Method: Web offset

Fonts: Edideic Modern, Eidedic Neo by
Rodrigo X. Cavazos
Photographers: Karl Petzke, Navid Baraty
Editor: Lindsey Westbrook
Writer: Alexis Raymond

Designer's Statement:

The viewbook highlights key messages about
the college's mission and values and has
information about majors, alumni, and student
profiles. The design is visually dense to give an
impression of the energy and vibrant culture
of CCA.

Title: SWA 2011 Wish Book
Firm: Aufuldish & Warinner
Designer: Bob Aufuldiner
Client: SWA Group
Client Industry: Landscape Architecture

Printer: Strahm Communications
Method: Offset

Fonts: Tribute by Frank Heine; National by
Kris Sowersby
Editor: Scott Cooper

Designer's Statement:

Each year, SWA sends out a new year's
announcement; the announcements relate
to the landscape in some way but never
show examples of SWA's work. For 2011,
the announcement was a brochure of details
of clouds enlarged from an encyclopedia of
engravings. The clouds are paired with quotes
that relate to nature and design. A list of
all the members of SWA runs along the edge
of the pages.

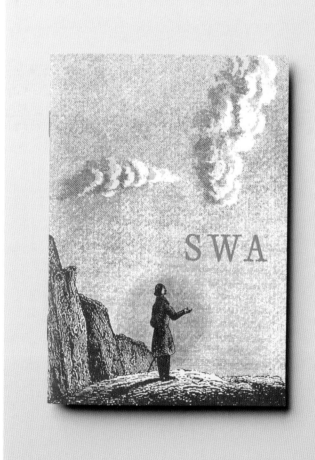

Title: Vista
Firm: Aufuldish & Warinner
Designer: Bob Aufuldish
Client: SWA Group
Client Industry: Landscape Architecture

Printer: Strahm Communications
Method: Offset

Font: National by Kris Sowersby
Photographer: Bob Aufuldish
Editor: Scott Cooper

Designer's Statement:

SWA's 2012 New Year's announcement was a brochure of evocative place names and landscape details photographed off monitor. A list of all the members of SWA runs along the edge of the pages.

Title: Mai Venga Il Mattino 7 Festival
Internazioinale Di Letteratura Chiasso
Firm: CCRZ
Art Director: Marco Cassino
Designer: Marco Cassino
Client: Festival Internazionale di
Letteratura Chiasso

Printers: Centro Stampa Ticino (newspaper),
Progetto Stampa (others)
Methods: Rotary press (newspaper) offset,
(postcard and ticket), digital (playbill), offset +
silkscreen (program)
Color: Fluorescent ink

Designer's Statement:

Companion pieces—prints for an International
Festival of Literature

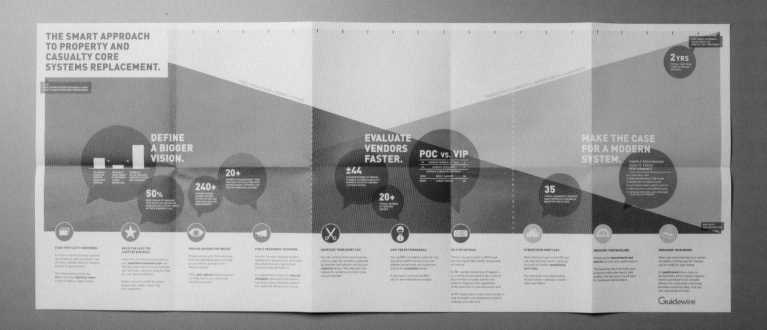

Title: Guidewire
Firm: C2 Group LLC
Art Director: Greg Galle
Designer: Kelsey Ann Lesko
Client: Guidewire
Client Industry: Software

Printer: Print Smart
Method: Offset, on packing paper
Color: 4 color + 5 process

Font: DinPro
Strategists: Greg Galle, Sarah Thorpe
Writer: Rich Binell

Designer's Statement:

Insurance companies rely on software like
the rest of us. To handle claims. To figure out
billing. To manage policies. If the right systems
aren't in place, it's a complete nightmare. And
finding the right system (and the right partner
to implement that system) is a shopping head-
ache. Guidewire creates software that builds
these smart systems.

Title: De Hallen Haarlem series
Firm: Cobbenhagen Hendriksen
Designers: Marijke Cobbenhagen and Chantal
Hendriksen
Client: De Hallen Haarlem
Client Industry: Arts/Culture

Printer: Lenoirschuring, Amstelveen, NL
Method: Offset, sometimes with HKS colors
instead of Pantone
Paper: Signature 80 gr/m2

Designer's Statement:

The identity of the contemporary art museum
De Hallen Haarlem functions on different levels.
The museum is built out of a composition of
three neighboring buildings on the Grote Markt
in Haarlem. This inspired us to start breaking up
fonts and after several drafts we were cutting
vertically into every possible typeface. Now we
could use a different typeface for every artist to
create his or her personal identity, and to visually connect him or her with the exhibition and
the De Hallen Haarlem. The intervention in the
typefaces makes De Hallen Haarlem recogniz-
able into its smallest detail and, at same time,
gives us the ultimate freedom to play around
with the overall identity.

CURIOUS**WORK**

Title: Curious Work
Firm: Curious
Designer: Louise Desborough
Client: Curious
Client Industry: Design

Printer: Concertina
Method: Litho

Designer's Statement:
Self-promotional mailer showcasing the best of Curious's work in an engaging format.

"I didn't know a great crested newt could stop a JCB"

CARTER JONAS

Title: For every shot a story.
Firm: Design Ranch
Client: Life Uncommon Photography
Client Industry: Photography

BREATHE. ARE THE FLOWERS SET? CHECK. WEDDING
PARTY? HERE. DID LINDA REMEMBER TO SET OUT
THE PLACE CARDS? THIS TICKLES. WHAT IF I RUIN MY
MAKEUP? IF DAD CRIES, I'M A LOST CAUSE. BREATHE.
DID I PUT ENOUGH HAIRSPRAY IN MY HAIR? IT HAS TO
HOLD ALL NIGHT. I'M GETTING MARRIED. I'M GETTING
MARRIED! I CAN'T WAIT TO START OUR LIVES TOGETHER.
THERE IS NO DOUBT IN MY MIND THAT HE IS THE ONE.
TODAY WILL BE PERFECT.

TIME, I'LL SCREAM. W
TIE? I HOPE MOM LET
BET THE CAKE IS CH
OVER YET? THIS JAC
A MOVE AT THE REC
UNCLE CHARLIE MY
"CRAZY TURTLE". I L

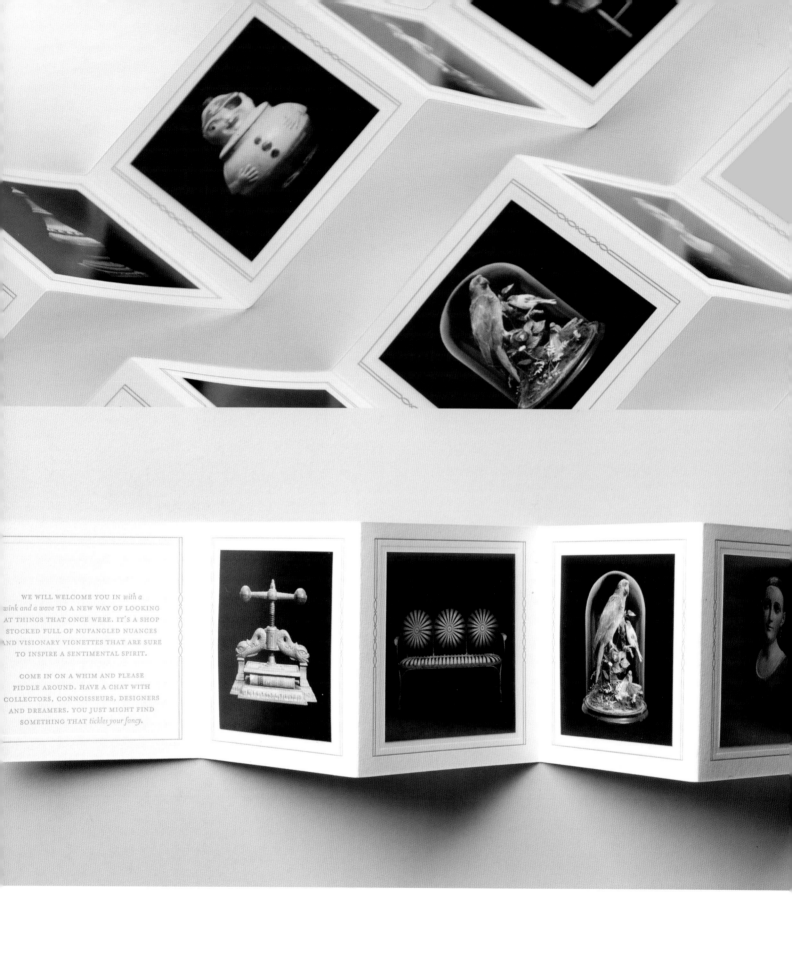

WE WILL WELCOME YOU IN *with a wink and a wave* TO A NEW WAY OF LOOKING AT THINGS THAT ONCE WERE. IT'S A SHOP STOCKED FULL OF NUFANGLED NUANCES AND VISIONARY VIGNETTES THAT ARE SURE TO INSPIRE A SENTIMENTAL SPIRIT.

COME IN ON A WHIM AND PLEASE FIDDLE AROUND. HAVE A CHAT WITH COLLECTORS, CONNOISSEURS, DESIGNERS AND DREAMERS. YOU JUST MIGHT FIND SOMETHING THAT *tickles your fancy.*

Title: Nufangle
Firm: Design Ranch
Client: Nufangle Antiques
Client Industry: Product/Retail

Title: The Collection—Emigre Type Library
Firm: Emigre
Art Director: Rudy VanderLans
Designer: Rudy VanderLans
Client: Emigre
Client Industry: Typography

Printer: American Web
Method: Web offset
Paper: 60 lb American Web Recycled Matte
Color: 4 color

Fonts: Emigre Fonts
Photographer: Rudy VanderLans
Illustrator: Rudy VanderLans
Writer: Rudy VanderLans

Designer's Statement:

Type specimens need not be limited to stacked
and justified compositions of arbitrary words
and phrases. Although the text is necessarily
subservient in the typographic exercise, there's
no reason to neglect the content. This type
specimen catalog encompasses the analysis
of a record collection, a series of seventeen
architectural photographs of historically significant buildings and sites in Los Angeles, and
a selection of anecdotal quotes about music
recording. It fuses these disparate elements
into a visual presentation serving the dual purpose of showcasing selections from the Emigre
Type Library while providing a story that can be
enjoyed like a nice goblet of wine.

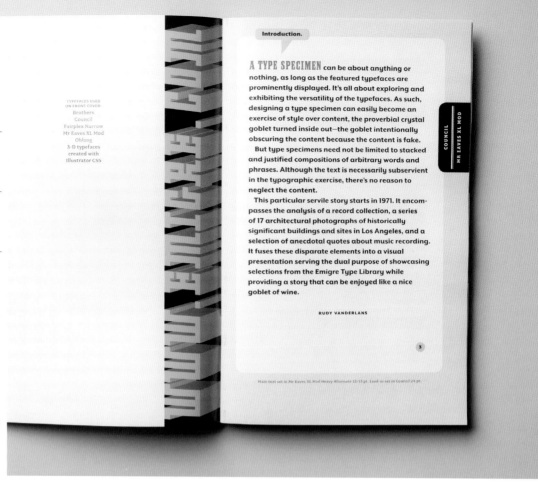

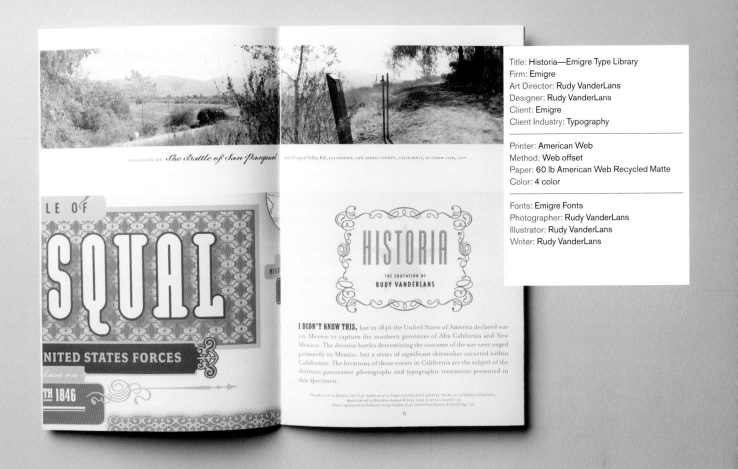

Title: Historia—Emigre Type Library
Firm: Emigre
Art Director: Rudy VanderLans
Designer: Rudy VanderLans
Client: Emigre
Client Industry: Typography

Printer: American Web
Method: Web offset
Paper: 60 lb American Web Recycled Matte
Color: 4 color

Fonts: Emigre Fonts
Photographer: Rudy VanderLans
Illustrator: Rudy VanderLans
Writer: Rudy VanderLans

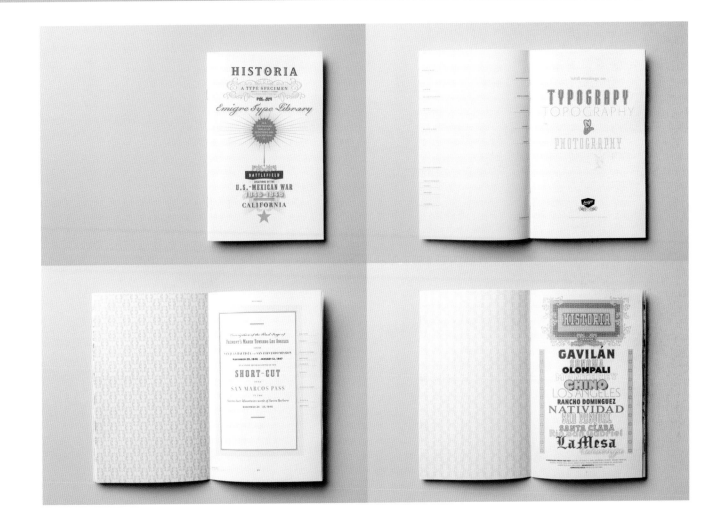

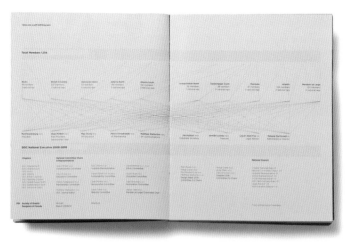

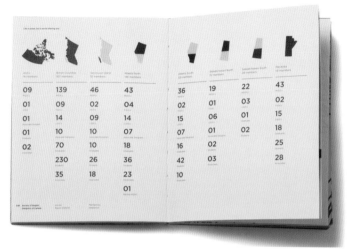

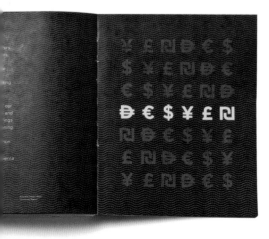

Title: Society of Graphic Designers of Canada
Annual Report
Firm: Foundry Communications
Art Director: Zahra Al-Harazi
Designers: Kylie Henry, Janice Wong, Jake Lim,
Jon Jungwirth
Client: Society of Graphic Designers of
Canada (GDC)

Printer: Blanchette Press
Illustrators: Kylie Henry, Janice Wong, Jake Lim,
Jon Jungwirth, Emmanuel Obayemi
Writer: Kitty Wong

Designer's Statement:

The GDC Annual needed to build upon
the sustainability rhetoric. We weaved the
sustainability conversation throughout the
book and dedicated one chapter to asking the
reader what it means to be sustainable within
the design industry through typographical
illustrations. In order to show the concept of
sustainability, we produced the book entirely on
make-readies and printed it using only two spot
colors. To allow the annual to be distinct, we uti-
lized a number of production elements, such as
untrimmed signature binding, exposed smyth-
sewn binding, and an unusual format—all of
which were informed by sustainable practices.
As a value add, each annual includes a poster
with all the member names printed on it.

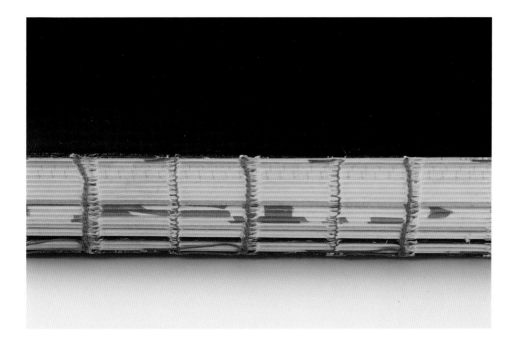

Title: Glifo promo
Firm: Glifo Associati s.c. (Milano, Italy)
Art Director: Fabiane Calonga
Designers: Fabiane Calonga (3D typography and layout), Francesco E. Guida (concept)
Client: Glifo Associati s.c.
Client Industry: Design/Communication/Typography

Printer: Arti grafiche Bianca & Volta (Truccazzano – Milano, Italy)
Method: Offset
Paper: Munken Lynx by Artic Paper
Colors: 4 colors (CMYK) + 1 special color (Pantone 807) + transparent gloss coating

Fonts: Univers, Bodoni, Times, Frutiger, Eckmann, Helvetica
Photographer: Fabiane Calonga
Writers: Francesco E. Guida, Dalila Freddi

Designer's Statement:

A glyph is the basic element of writing. To design means to organize and give an order to informations and shapes. The basic element of design is typography. Glyphs are basic elements of the graphic design process.

For the new series of promotional cards for the Glifo Milan-based design studio, the concept was the centrality of typography in the design process, starting from the term *glyph* (*glifo* in Italian). Utilizing it to describe some of the most important acts of design with the following keywords and to compose the word *glifo* itself: glyph (*glifo*), language (*linguaggio*), information (*informazione*), figuration (*figurazione*), order (*ordine*).

The different visual subjects are emphasized by using different types (of different ages and styles), print effects (diecut, special color, transparent gloss coating) or by photos of 3D handmade typo-compositions.

The three series work as single folds or as indipendent cards series.

On the covers, three citations from Federico Fellini (film director), Francesco De Sanctis (philosopher) and Achille Castiglioni (designer) complete the description of Glifo's overall approach to design.

Energy Efficiency Programs
COMMERCIAL AND INSTITUTIONAL MARKET

Take the Challenge

477 participants in Gazifère's energy efficiency programs for commercial and institutional customers

1 709 401 m³ of natural gas saved

3251 tons of green house gas emissions avoided

Gazifère counted on persuading more of its commercial and institutional customers to buy into a business philosophy that puts energy efficiency first.

This guide is intended as an invitation to take the challenge with us.

Gazifère

706 boulevard Gréber
Gatineau (QC) J8V 3P8
Telephone 819 771-8321
Fax 819 771-8680
gazifere.com

USE heating of
domestic hot water only

WATER HEATER →

Outcome of a group effort

Energy Efficiency Programs
COMMERCIAL AND INSTITUTIONAL MARKET

OUR
2001-2009
RESULTS →

FEASIBILITY STUDY

Before you renovate or expand, have a feasibility study done to learn what measures are available to improve the energy performance of your building. This will demonstrate a proactive approach to staying competitive.

Gazifère offers financial assistance of $2,000 for an energy assessment completed by an engineering firm.

Looking to build?

Commission an energy simulation (using EE4 or Génie EE software) in order to qualify for $2,000 in financial support

...performed as se...
...source other th...
...ose measures ...
...has already gra...
...ization must n...
...e recommendat...

Check the Statement of Work at **gazifere.com**

Financial support from Gazifère

Mail us a summary of the feasibility study or e... simulation report.

The provision of financial assistance by Gazifè... conditional on the customer's participation in ... evaluation of the program.

Title: Gazifère
Firm: Gontran Blais Design
Art Director: Gontran Blais
Designer: Gontran Blais
Client: Gazifère
Client Industry: Energy

Printer: Imprimerie DuProgrès
Color: 3 color

Title: Hatch 2011 Easter Egg Coloring Kit
Firm: Hatch Design
Art Directors: Katie Jain, Joel Templin
Designer: Jeffrey Bucholtz

Method: Offset and flocking

Designer's Statement:

Annually since 2008, Hatch Design has been holding an Easter egg coloring contest, welcoming participants to enter their egg designs from all over the world.

What fun! For everyone. Elevating the easter egg decoration kit to a design showpiece. It's promotional in the best way possible—engaging creativity and community building.

Plus, we're jealous. We've always wanted to do a project with flocking.

Title: Hatch 2010 Easter Egg Coloring Kit
Firm: Hatch Design
Art Directors: Katie Jain, Joel Templin
Designer: Eszter Clark

There's something about annual traditions—something you can count on, but with inspiring variety, and in the case of easter egg decorating, limitless possibilities.

Title: In brief.
Firm: hat-trick design
Art Directors: Jim Sutherland, Gareth Howat
Designer: Alexandra Jurva
Client: hat-trick (Self-promotional)
Client Industry: Design (promo)

Printer: 1010 Printing International Ltd
Paper: Gold East Matte art paper 80 gsm,
section sewn, separate ends, case in Baladek
(black) over 1.5 mm Board H/T bands B&W

Font: Helvetica Neue
Writer: Nick Asbury

Designer's Statement:
To celebrate our 10th anniversary, we decided
to produce a small book, *In Brief.*

OBJECTIVES
The aim was to showcase and celebrate some
of our work from the past ten years. From a
list of over 1,000 projects, we had the task of
condensing it down to 146 that would make it
into the book. Each project comes with a very
brief description, written by Nick Asbury, as we
feel that the work should speak for itself.

The book opens with a quote by Elmore
Leonard: "I try to leave out the parts that people
skip." This is closely followed by the four-word
foreword: "Briefs aren't. Ideas are."

**Very small, but full of our favorite type of
work—exuberant and entertaining.**

**And thick . . . no page numbers, but we're
guessing 512 pages.**

Intriguing headlines lead into cool projects.

Title: **In brief.**
Firm: hat-trick design

Actual size!

We just love this little book. It showcases
the work, but even more, it conveys
the thinking and the personality of the firm.
As intended, it speaks for itself.

Title: Working in partnership:
Reaching five by fifteen
Firm: hat-trick design
Art Directors: Jim Sutherland, Gareth Howat
Designer: Adam Giles
Client: Marie Stopes International
Client Industry: Non-profit

Printer: Boss print
Method: Litho
Papers: 100 gsm matte art (text), 200 gsm
matte art (cover)
Colors: 4 color with spot gloss and matte
varnishes

Fonts: Folio, Helvetica Neue
Photographer: Various
Writers: Scott Perry

Designer's Statement:

Marie Stopes International (MSI) was looking
for an identity for its new campaign called "Five
by Fifteen." It's a global campaign aimed at
decision makers around the world, highlighting
the impact MSI has.

OBJECTIVES

Why Five? The United Nations Millennium
Development Goal 5 calls for a reduction in the
maternal mortality ratio by three-quarters and
universal access to reproductive health.

Why Fifteen? That's the deadline. 2015 is the
target date to achieve this goal.

DESIGN STRATEGY

It is all based around doors, and the MSI logo,
and on the idea of access for all. The aim of
the campaign was vast but the budget to
produce collateral was small. We had to ensure
that everything worked as hard as it could.
We produced three booklets and three viral
films, setting out the story, accompanied by
a soundtrack we had composed and played
on wooden doors. The website includes an
"impact calculator" which is a way of accessing
statistics and numbers from around the world
by country. This was a key part of this project,
as the numbers and access of them is fundamental to realizing the extent of the problem.
We also produced full-size adhesive doors and
key rings for events.

INSIDE

Title: Sweet Spot/Bridgewater Emeryville
Firm: Hutner Descollonges
Art Director: Justine Descollonges
Designer: Evelyn Liu
Client: iStar Financial
Client Industry: Real Estate

Printer: Oscar Printing
Method: Offset
Colors: 4 color + 1 spot

Designer's Statement:

Real estate brochure for first-time home buyers looking to purchase a condominium in Emeryville, CA.

SWEET SPOT.

BRIDGEWATER

The American Dream meets the Age of Reason.

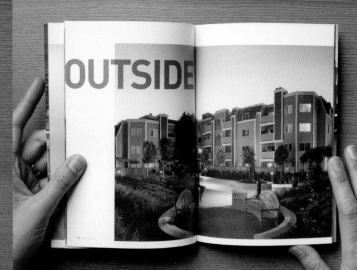

OUTSIDE

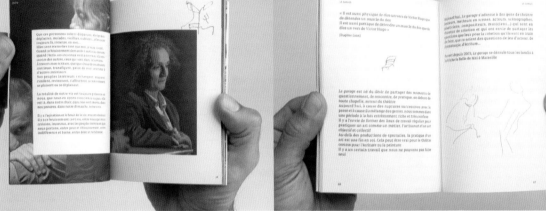

Title: Compagnie L'Entreprise (François Cervantès, Marseille)

Firm: Johann Hierholzer

Client: Compagnie L'Entreprise (Marseilles)

Method: Offset

Paper: Olin Extra Blanc (120 g)

Photographers: Christophe Raynaud de Lage, Xavier Brousse

Designer's Statement:

The theatrical Compagnie L'Entreprise created by François Cervantes (author and director) is based in "La Friche La Belle de Mai" in Marseilles. The company plays with its band, performing his repertoire all over France and abroad. Each year a new program reflects the new designs and plays of the repertoire that will be played on tour. The die cut in the cover was originally intended to represent a small window illuminated by the company, in the vast complex of La Friche. Since then, it has allowed a graphic game between the exterior and the interior; the illustrations of the cover page evolve according to the latest creations of the company.

Title: Compagnie Les Carboni (Marseille)
Firm: Johann Hierholzer
Client: Compagnie Les Carboni (Marseille)

Method: Offset
Paper: Cyclus print

Designer's Statement:

The Festival of "13 paniers" (The Panier: historical district of Marseilles) created by Carboni and led by Fred Muhl Valentin, meets both fairground theater and street music, in an itinerant scenic structure: La Posada.

The photo montage brings a surrealist gap, evokes humor, and pluridisciplinary arts, the association of different artists, and the assembly and disassembly of the arena with unlikely cinematic elements in the middle. Everything seems as removable as the structure itself.

Title: Southern Exposure/Oct. 2011–
Jan. 2012
Firm: MacFadden & Thorpe
Art Director: Scott Thorpe
Designer: Scott Thorpe
Client: Southern Exposure
Client Industry: Arts/Culture

Printer: Oscar Printing
Method: Offset
Paper: White 80-lb stock
Color: 2 color

Designer's Statement:

Folded poster/announcement for a group show
in which each artist creates her project in the
gallery during conventional working hours. The
announcement folds down into a small pocket-
able size, and unfolded, uses rules to divide the
piece into a cubical-farm like diagram. On the
poster side, text overprints a highlighter yellow
photograph of a stereotypical modern office,
with rows of cubicles and fluorescent lights.

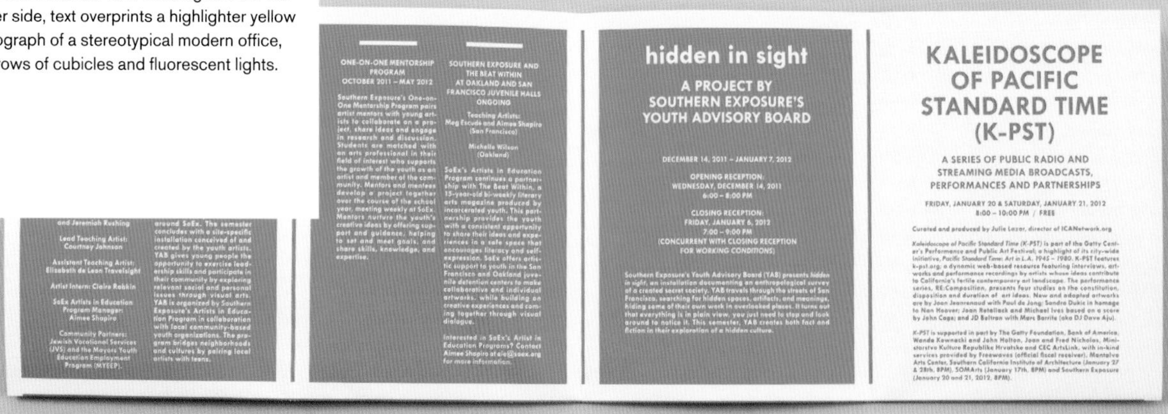

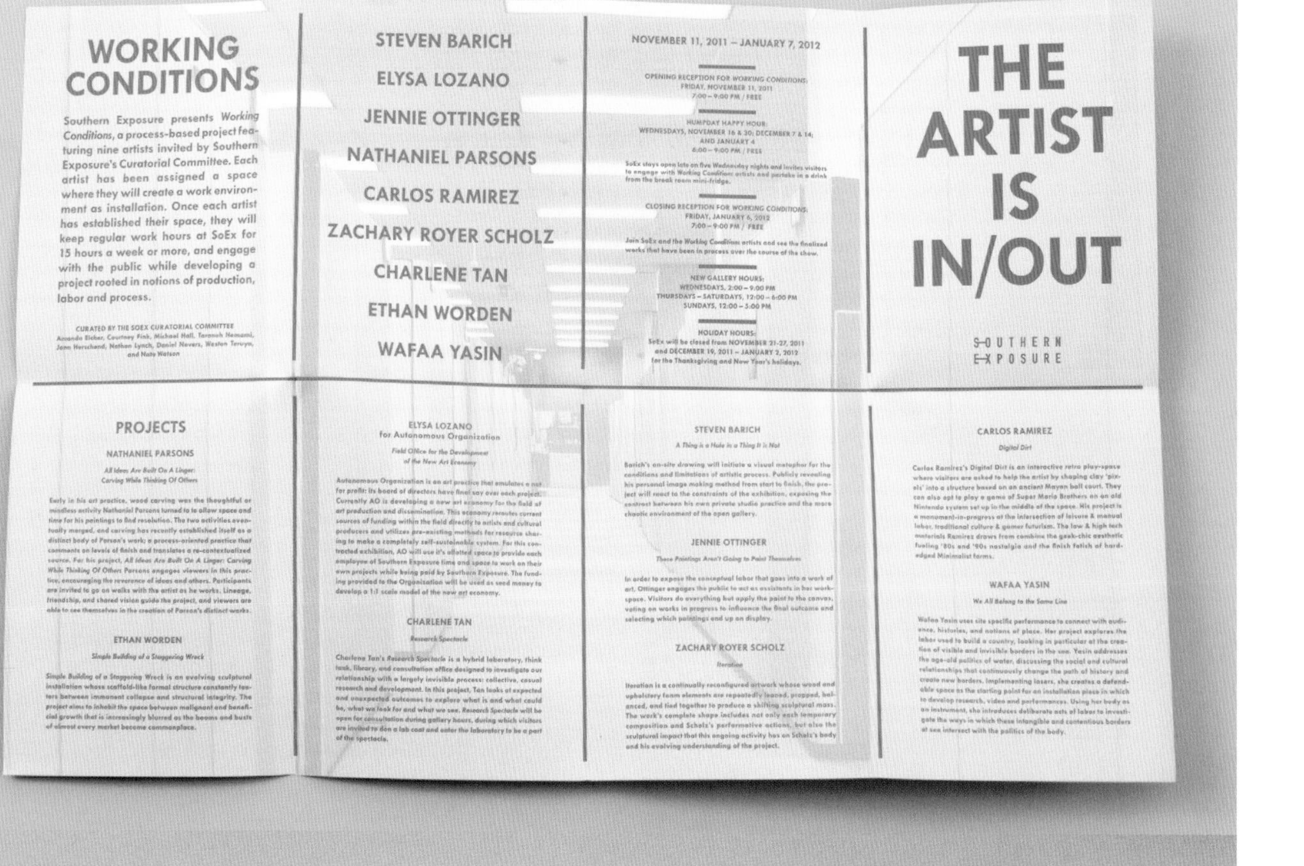

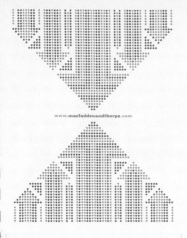

www.macfaddenandthorpe.com

FEBRUARY

Through the early winter, we dug into one of our most personal projects to date: *Hot Type*, a book of 30 typographic iron-on fabric transfers. These fun sayings and cut-and-compose alphabets let you personalize your gear as you like. We got really into the project, and ended up delivering nearly twice the drawings contracted—close to 60—which means we are well prepared for *Hot Type the Sequel, Too Hot to Stop*. Look for *Hot Type* from Chronicle Books in October 2009, and don't be shy about buying them for all your friends. Lord knows we need the royalties.

And on that note, we find ourselves at the end of our first year's wrap-up. We thank you for your interest and support and look forward to another year making beautiful graphic design together. Our best wishes for you and yours, many happy returns, Brett & Scott.

Hot Type allows you to iron-on snappy typographic sayings to your cherished garments. Included alphabets allow you to cut out letters to spell things like your name, your favorite band, or outrageous

1

MacFadden & Thorpe Yearbook
2008.03–2009.03

Title: Dreams Made Real
Firm: MacFadden & Thorpe
Art Directors: Brett MacFadden, Scott Thorpe
Designers: Brett MacFadden, Scott Thorpe
Client: Self-Initiated
Client Industry: Graphic Design

Printer: Technigraphics
Method: Offset
Paper: White 80-lb stock
Color: 2 color

Designer's Statement:

A small booklet about our first year in business, highlighting projects, adventures, and friends made. For economy's sake, it was printed as a double-sided poster that was folded down, trimmed, and stapled (the last part by us) in order to make the book. Red and Blue—our company colors—were used along with over-printing to create a third, purple.

JANUARY

A 170-square-foot studio can be many things: cozy, efficient, easy to vacuum. But it can also just be small. So when the opportunity arose to move to a 1000+ sq.ft. space in the museum district, we packed up our Pantone® books® and went downtown.

Soon enough we started work on an identity for Society Creative—an industrial design consultancy. Matt Boyko, their principal, wanted a logo that was straightforward and spoke to the tactical and thoughtful nature of the work they produce. As we evaluated early schemes, Matt suggested incorporating a QR code, which can be scanned and translated by a cell phone camera (right). Within the pattern of the code, we extracted shapes to form the firm's initials and this became the logo. The front of each business card has standard contact info; while the backside features the QR code plus translations into Chinese, Japanese, and Korean.

SocietyCreative

The Society Creative logo forms out of this QR code and is embossed through the paper to read right on the front. If you scan this code with a QR reader on your cell phone it will link you to the studio's website.

APRIL

In April, we created an identity for Kevin Gulley's company Green Collar, which helps companies gain from greener business practices. We also started an ongoing relationship with the Boys & Girls Club of San Francisco, starting with the design of their 2007 Annual Report, and continuing with a number of projects throughout the year (and coming full circle as we begin work on their 2009 report this month).

Our copywriter friend Jenn Shreve contacted us about designing her website—using sentence structure diagrams for the navigation (right). Now the site is up (www.jennshreve.com) and she's making loads of money writing jingles in New York City.

The Future Starts Here

GREEN COLLAR

Our new studio finds us conveniently in the thick of downtown, with lovely Yerba Buena gardens nearby for Brett to sleep in while Scott sweats it out in the studio.

Custom typography was employed in Southern Exposure's annual greeting to their member community.

B.&G. Club

Love SOUTHERN EXPOSURE

DECEMBER

Winter in San F... some rain if it's ... of rain if not. Wi... which for Scott ... year in Tahoe.® ... November was ... saw Scott on a ...

During that ti... at Southern Ex... an extremely ... asked us if we ... fitting New Yea... organization.

We wanted to ... playful that rep... common optim... a rough few yea... that had becom... economically. W... card that double... stickers, where ... words Happy, A... 2009, and Love... out and given a l... The card was well-recieved, by all accounts, and we're pleased to continue our connection with SOEX for their inaugural show as they move to a beautiful new space this summer.

by Coffee Miklos from 2008 (top) with considerably more firepower.

's: ...
Now ...
To-...
Georgia

F I X U R E

THE THING ISSUES 2, 3.5, 4, 5, 6

This past year we enjoyed assisting *The Thing* with design to accompany pieces by Anne Walsh (2), Tucker Nichols (3.5), Trisha Donelley (4), Lucy Pullen (5), and Allora & Calzadilla (6).

The Thing also gave us the opportunity to continue collaborating with our friend Tucker Nichols when they asked us to help with a promotional piece they made for the New York Art Book Fair. Tucker's *Free Map* (shown in background and at right) is a map to nowhere (or everywhere).

FREE MAP

COMPLI-MENTS OF THE THING

B

Extruded metal letters form the elegant new dimensional signage for the San Bruno Public Library.

OCTOBER

Brett's birthday is October 26, just, you know, in case you want to send balloons.

For the San Francisco Museum of Modern Art (SFMOMA), we produced a typographic illustration for their member's magazine. At right we adapted the ribbon-maze type from that piece for a new phrase.

The sweetest month in San Francisco also brought the long-awaited final installation of our San Bruno Public Library signage project. A small city south of SF, San Bruno has a cool row of mid-century modern® municipal buildings, including the library, a fire station, City Hall, and an adjacent school. As part of a larger planned renovation for the 1954 building, we were brought in to amplify the signage, while keeping it architecturally consistent with the structure's era. A 20-foot wide stainless-steel sign was added to the facade, and a 10-foot wide one hung from the main entrance awning (left).

AUGUST

BLDGBLOG is a popular website that broadly explores the world of architecture, landscape, and our urban enviornment. Working with Geoff Manaugh, the blog's author, we designed a book that expanded on some of the site's areas of investigation, from underground installations to controlling the weather. When it came time to consider the cover, Geoff encouraged us to stroll far and wide. We explored what the cover might be if it were a flag for a fictional country, or if it were a record album. What if the cover were made up of all the basic graphic elements we could use to design the book? or if the stars conspired to publicise the project? The amazing drawing at left shows one sketch, where we proposed an architectural illustrator could render the logo as a building, complete with runway, hot-air balloon, subway, nuclear missile silo, skyscraper, habitable lightning, and a swing over a ship. Sadly, this superb design solution was snuffed early in the review process.

Two of the many covers considered for *The BLDG-BLOG Book*: "Kit of Parts" and "Constellation."

BLDG BLOG

WAIT, THERE'S MORE

WE MAKE IT EASY

DREAMS MADE REAL

MacFadden & Thorpe
Graphic Design

ESTAB-LISHED 2008

We love all the unusual, funky, homemade typefaces—
especially enhanced with patterns.

Two spot colors with overprinting—
it's an art form.

MACFADDEN & THORPE is the graphic des[ign]
studio of Brett MacFadden and Scott Thorpe.
We work with a variety of clients and collabo[rate]
on print, digital, and environmental projects.
We approach each project with an earnest b[elief]
in partnership, and the ability of design to in[form]
and clarify. We aspire to create work that is
smart, functional, and handsome, regardles[s of]
medium, budget, or market. We both previo[usly]
worked at Chronicle Books in San Francisco,
where Brett was Senior Designer in the Art [&]
Design category, and Scott headed the Mark[eting]
Design Group. We each hold MFA's in Desig[n,]
Scott from the Rhode Island School of Desig[n,]
Brett from the Cranbrook Academy of Art.

Our motto, provided by our friend and clien[t]
Tucker Nichols, is: "We Make It Easy."

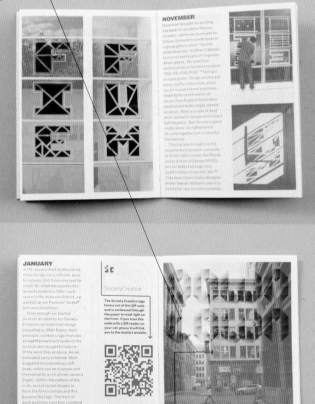

NOVEMBER

JANUARY

SocietyCreative

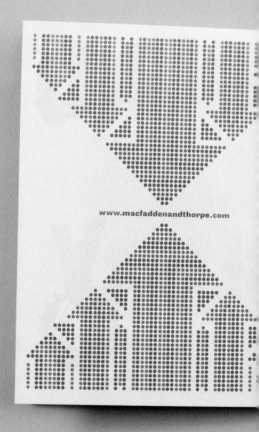

www.macfaddenandthorpe.com

Title: Dreams Made Real
Firm: MacFadden & Thorpe

OCTOBER

Brett's birthday is Octo[...]
just, you know, in case y[...]
send balloons.[12]

For the San Francisco Museum of Modern Art (SFMOMA), we produced a typographic illustration for their member's magazine. At right we adapted the ribbon-maze type from that piece for a new phrase.

The sweetest month in San Francisco also brought the long-awaited final installation of our San Bruno Public Library signage project. A small city south of SF, San Bruno has a cool row of mid-century modern[13] municipal buildings, including the library, a fire station, City Hall, and an adjacent school. As part of a larger planned renovation for the 1954 building, we were brought in to amplify the signage, while keeping it architecturally consistent with the structure's era. A 20-foot wide stainless-steel sign was added to the facade, and a 10-foot wide one hung from the main entrance awning (left).

Extruded metal letters form the elegant new dimensional signage for the San Bruno Public Library.

The writing is a nice balance of promotion and personality. It creates a soft sell vibe that sets these guys apart from a typical design firm.

adden & Thorpe Yearbook
03–2009.03

K YOU

to thank the
family, clients
ners that
s prepare for
vive our first
usiness. One
eat joys of
rprise is the
ou are exposed
e way they
and help
hat develops.
hk those we've
with and
ward to those
ome.

dden Family
Family
nna MacFadden
Wagner
"Maybelle"

ams
azawa
lita
Bagnato
iley
arnhurst
ark
ue
Bober
w Boyko
randt
Brown
a Bruxvoort
ine Bullimore
Callahan

Brendan Callahan
Denise Cante
Michael Carabetta
Cardoza–James Bindery
Anna Carollo
Michelle Clair
Jenna Cushner
Andrew Dahley
Nick de la Mare
Vanessa Dina
El Tonayense Taco Truck
Doria Fan
Courtney Fink
Jacob Gardner
Meg Geer
Pamela Geismar
Cary Gibaldi
Michael Goldberg
Lisa Hamilton
DJ Harmon
Guinevere Harrison
Ed Hatter, CPA
Daniell Hebert
Jonn Herschend
Laura Heyenga
Cavan Huang
Greg Janess
Brittany Johnson
Brooke Johnson
Tracy Johnson
Ben Kasman
Tera Killip
David Lawrence
Eloise Leigh
Alice Lin
Sarah Malarkey
Geoff Manaugh
Peter Medilek
Cheryl Meeker
Sabrina Merlo
Lindsay Metcalfe

Alethea Morrison
Tucker Nichols
Susie Nielsen
Margeigh Novotny
Kerry O'Grady
Mary Hallam Pearse
Alan Rapp
Liz Rico
Carl Robertson
Will Rogan
Josh Rubinstein
Sara Schneider
Mike Shay
Suzette Sherman
Ilona Sherratt
Jenn Shreve
Jennifer Sonderby
Marianna Stark
Peter Stathis
Mike Stewart
John Sueda
TechniGraphics Printing
John Tosch
Julia Turner
Rick Vargas
Martin Venezky
Tim Wallace
Watermark Press
Bridget Payne Watson
Maysoun Wazwaz
West Coast Signworks
Jo Whaley
Kate Woodrow
Bart Wright
Alan Zhu, CPA

We'd especially like to thank **PMS Red 032**, PMS 2995, and the typeface **Maple** for their valued service.

NOTES

1. For two years Brett & Scott sat back to back, now we sit side by side at the same desk. Progress!

2. Mike Stewart and Brett shared a tiny dorm room in grad school. Not by choice.

3. In order to expand the capabilities of MT's in-house courier service, Brett put a big basket on his bike. He learned that it's neither easy nor safe to ride with a six-pack in it.

4. No, we don't have a MT yacht.

5. This was Scott's 2nd Marathon. Whatev.

6. Issues 7–10 will include works by Jonathan Lethem, Trevor Paglen, Ryan Gander, and Starlee Kine.

7. Brett saw a sign for a lost dog named Taco. Brett is mad for tacos. So he decided to help with the effort and redesigned and posted new signs. We hope Taco is back home safe.

8. Photographer Gretchen LaMaistre took a portrait of Maybelle the dog, in return for using Brett's apartment as a location for a book called XXX Porn for Women.

9. Stars!

10. For one thing that bike weighs about 60 pounds. It's absurd.

11. Mike Essi is not actually a butcher, but his studio is called ME/AT.

12. Scott's Birthday was June 23rd and Brett made him a gold-leaf letter "T" on glass.

13. The Libary was built in 1954 and designed by William T. Rowe.

14. The window was made of four columns of 5 panes each, so Fee Fie Foe Fum, fit very nicely.

15. Scott and Brett grew up in adjacent Massachusetts towns, but didn't know each other until meeting at Chronicle.

16. '08–09 Tahoe snowfall = 468 in. @ 8200 ft elv.

17. We ♥ So-Ex.

18. And a lot of other crap.

19. Seriously.

20. Thank you for reading (or skimming). We know you're busy and we appreciate it.

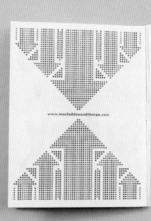

LUXURY

Julia Hoffmann
Museum of Modern Art
New York, New York

In today's age, printing has become a luxury. While budgets have been cut and environmental consciousness has risen, clients often default to emails or electronic flyers. For designers, it's a shame. The workload is usually the same, if not more, but the results aren't as tangible. Designers long for the ephemeral quality of print work, such as the opportunity to select a paper and make folding prototypes. That's why the design of brochures has been getting better. At MoMA, where the grab rate of any printed material is 30 percent, we have to be conscious of what we put out there. With almost 3 million visitors a year, a lot of brochures end up on the floor of the lobby and throughout the museum at the end of a busy day. This reality resulted in a drastic cut of printed materials. Regardless, and luckily, there are plenty of other opportunities to rethink brochures and distribute them in places where they're least expected. For example, our team came up with a zine for an exhibition that was printed very cheaply on newsprint and then distributed in neighborhood cafés and bookstores, where people had time to browse. A zine seemed more effective and affordable than a small print ad in a daily newspaper.

Twice a year, the education department at MoMA offers a teen program with classes and workshops. With a tight budget, we have to work around some restrictions: The client wants a poster that schools can put on bulletin boards but simultaneously wants it to function as a brochure, listing all the different classes offered. We looked at school bulletins and realized that a big poster would take up too much space, and a brochure would get lost in the sea of advertising materials out there. So we settled on a vertical fold-out brochure with two sides, so that a school could pin up each side and still have enough room for other announcements. Because our printing budget was limited, we used colored paper to add an extra color, which made the poster/brochure stand out visually even more.

Once we settled on this format, we assigned the project to our current intern, who gets briefed directly by the client about the content of the upcoming courses and activities (every year the teen program has a loosely connected theme). The basic type styles are already set; however, each brochure needs some amount of retypesetting and rearranging of text based on the new content. Underneath the text layer, the interns explore a wide range of aesthetic and conceptual treatments relating to the course selection. We like to experiment with technical printing techniques such as using two- and three-color printing, colored paper, overprinting, or unusual Pantone color combinations. Our interns always have different backgrounds and aesthetic strengths, and we like to push unique, fun, and experimental illustration and pattern options. This has proven to be a perfect teaching tool for young designers. We love that this process works well for a series, but that each intern is unique. The intern, who is usually still a student in college, works on the project from start to finish, and learns about client relationships, concept development, typesetting, and production. Our portfolio benefits from the different personalities at work. It's a win-win situation.

Julia

Artlog: MoMA Teens series
Firm: Department of Advertising and Graphic
Design, The Museum of Modern Art
Art Director: Sam Sherman
Creative Director: Julia Hoffmann
Production Manager: Althea Penza
Designer: Jesse Reed
Client: The Museum of Modern Art
Client Industry: Arts/Culture

Printer: Gemson
Method: Offset
Papers: Astrobrite 60 lb (text) colored paper
Accent Opaque 60 lb (text)
Colors: 2/2, 2 regular PMS or 1 PMS +
1 fluorescent PMS

Copy Editor: Rebecca Roberts

TEENS

MoMATEEN

TEE
NIGI

MoMATEENS

TE
NIG

MoMATEENS

ART

Prime example of using a template but creating unending variation. Using the same masthead and font maintains a consistent feel but mixing it up with color and imagery keeps things fresh and interesting.

Great use of two and three spot-color printing.

This series is fun and age appropriate for the audience. [Although, as an office of non-teens, we were universally excited and engaged!] When you see it as a series, it feels exciting but still holds up as individual pieces.

Artlog: MoMA Teens series
Firm: Department of Advertising and Graphic
Design, The Museum of Modern Art

Irreverance in a museum is definitively
modern. It is refreshing that pink and purple
are not out of the question, or that turning a
piece to read varying elements is OK.

The collection of objects is intriguing,
of the moment, youthful, and fun.

Title: Cesar Rubio Photography Promo
Firm: Public
Designer: Tessa Lee
Client: Cesar Rubio Photography
Client Industry: Photography

Printer: PS. PrintSmart/All City Printing
Method: Offset
Color: 4 color

Photographer: Cesar Rubio Photography

Designer's Statement:

A promotional piece that unfolds into
a poster

CESAR RUBIO
PHOTOGRAPHY
415
550 6369
cesarrubio.com

represented by
freda scott, inc.
415 349 9121
info@fredascott.com

Title: Sidecut Restaurant in-room promotional brochure
Firm: Public
Art Director: Todd Foreman
Designer: Todd Foreman
Client: Sidecut Restaurant
Client Industry: Hotel Restaurant

Printer: PS. PrintSmart/All City Printing
Method: Offset
Color: 4 color

Designer's Statement:

An in-room promotional piece for the restaurant at the Four Seasons Resort in Whistler, BC. This was part of a rebranding of the restaurant from a formal low-key venue to a casual steak house with fun bar and live entertainment.

Title: Coalesse brochure series
Firm: Tolleson
Creative Director: Steve Tolleson
Design Director: Molly Skonieczny
Designer: Boramee Seo
Production: Rene Rosso
Client: Coalesse
Client Industry: Cross-over furniture industry

Printer: QuadWillamson
Method: UV
Paper: Cougar Cover 80 lb smooth (cover),
Cougar Text 100 lb smooth (text)
Color: 6/6, 4 color + 2 PMS + AQ UV (cover
and text)

Fonts: Granjon, Aaux Pro, Helvetica Neue
Photographers: Eric Einwiller, Noah Webb
Illustrator: Sean Lee
Writer: Tony Leighton

Designer's Statement:
Designed specifically to launch Coalesse in
the EU at the Bavarian Days event, these high
production value booklets feature both setting
and individual product shots of the local offering. Introducing the cross-over, live/work story
to this new audience, they bring a California
sensibility to the European market.

**The exterior is simple, black printing on
white uncoated text-weight paper with an
intriguing fold (it slips into itself and holds
the piece together) evidenced by the layout
and cropping of type.**

**Opening the fold reveals a full color image
on coated cover stock.**

48

The nonadhesive package houses a series of postcards. It's a fun package.

A companion piece uses another folding format—this time, a poster housing a postcard collrection. Button included. Weird but cool.

Title: Coalesse brochure series
Firm: Tolleson

The unfolded folder/poster showcases various abstracted images of live/work. Great color and photography.

Title: Armando Museum Bureau
Firm: Vanessa van Dam
Designer: Vanessa van Dam
Client: Armando Museum/Yvonne Ploum
Client Industry: Arts/Culture

Printer: Virtual Printer
Font: Typeface 'Armando' designed by Vanessa
van Dam, David Bennewith

Designer's Statement:

It's unusual to have a museum named after
a living artist. It's more inviting and personal.
This was the starting point for me to give the
museum a personal signature, as if you receive
a handwritten letter. To underline this aspect
I developed, together with David Bennewith,
a new typeface, based on the principle of
what happens when you write with a marker
or (fountain) pen; the occurrence of a darker
spot where your pen lingers on the paper. Every
single character and punctuation mark has it's
most logical position for this spot and every
character has two or three variants (because
everybody writes differently).

FIN
ISS
AGE

AR
MAN
DO

MU
SE
UM

27
11
2011

ARMANDO
&

AARON
VAN ERP

10–10–2010 T/M
30–01–2011

ARMANDO MUSEUM
BUREAU

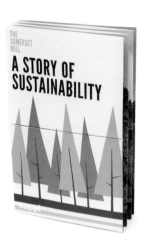

THE SOMERSET MILL

A STORY OF SUSTAINABILITY

Title: A Story of Sustainability
Firm: VSA Partners, Inc.
Designer: Brandt Brinkerhoff
Client: Sappi Fine Paper North America
Client Industry: Paper/Print

Printer: John Roberts Printing Company
Method: Conventional/Offset
Paper: Somerset Satin Text 80 lb (text) Opus Gloss 120 lb (cover)
Color: 4-color process, match blue, match orange plus overall satin aqueous

Photographer: Greg Hanrahan Photography (greghanrahan.com) & Getty Images

Designer's Statement:
Tucked away in the foothills of central Maine, Sappi's Somerset Mill has made its name as one of the largest coated paper mills in the world. But while its size and technological sophistication have fueled its reputation, the mill is fast becoming recognized as a model of sustainability. Led by a $36 million investment in a recovery boiler upgrade, Somerset is examining every single step of the papermaking process to find new ways to lower its carbon footprint. Interact with this brochure's unique fold, featured as Fold of the Week by Fold Factory (11/28/11), and integrated QR Code linking to a chaptered animation that brings the chemical recovery process to life on sappi.com/eQ.

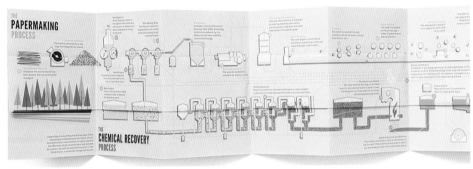

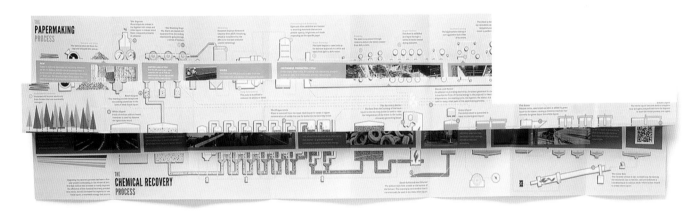

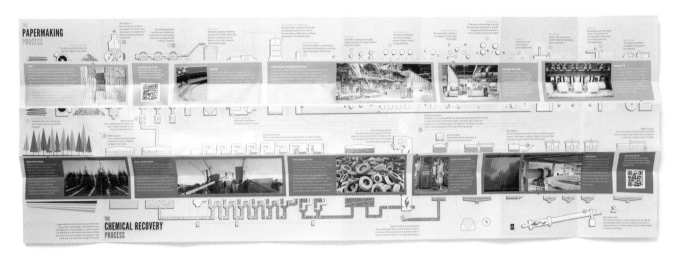

Title: 2010 Faculty Catalog
Firm: The Official Office of Art Director and
Designer: W. Anthony Watkins

Art Director: W. Anthony Watkins
Designer: W. Anthony Watkins
Client: Sam Houston State University
Department of Art
Client Industry: Education/Academia

Printer: Signature Media, Houston, TX
Method: Offset
Papers: Mohawk Via, Pure White Smooth 100
lb (cover), 80 lb (text)
Color: 4 color process

Designer's Statement:
Featuring the work of faculty from various creative disciplines, this catalog utilizes a simple column grid system to accommodate multiple as well as full–bleed images. Faculty were asked to provide a personal artistic statement as well as a third–person description of their accomplishments, which are differentiated by typeface and color. The catalog features a partially concealed spiral binding and french folded pages.

Title: Chromolux m-real
Firm: Zinnobergruen gmbh
Designer: Bärbel Muhlack, Tobias Schwarzer
Client: Metsä Board Zanders GmbH
Client Industry: Paper

Method: Offset and silkscreen printing
Paper: Chromolux board range
Color: 4 color (different Pantone colors)

Designer's Statement:
The Ideas Preserver is a handy tool to save ideas. Subdivided into six categories the user can save 72 ideas in total, each on one designated card. All cards are designed differently to demonstrate various creative solutions by using Chromolux board. As a permanent companion of the creative the ideas preserver supports the creative potential during the development of the idea on the board self.

A PHOTO LOG
TAKEN OVER THREE
DAYS DURING THE SO
CALLED 'BIG FREEZE'.
WHAT A GLORIOUS
WHITE SPECTACLE

Title: A Photo Log
Firm: Shout Design Associates
Art Director: Mark Benham
Client: Mark Benham
Client Industry: Design/Photography

Printer: RipeDigital
Method: Digital
Paper: Splendorgel

Photographer: Mark Benham
(markbenham.co.uk)

Designer's Statement:

A personal project to visually record heavy
snowfall in England, I designed a pocket-sized,
perfect bound booklet.

CRUNCHY SNOW
CRISP DAYS
AMAZING LIGHT
BLUE SKIES
RED NOSE

Artlog: California College of the Arts
Graduate Studies
Firm: Noon
Art Director: Cinthia Wen
Designer: Cinthia Wen
Client: California College of the Arts
Client Industry: Education/Academia

medium

Title: 57 Things
Firm: Adobe Brand Experience,
Adobe Systems, Inc.
Designers: Sam Wick, Shawn Cheris,
Sonja Hernandez

Client: Adobe Systems
Client Industry: Software

Printer: p.s. PrintSmart
Methods: Digital printed book block, two color
PMS offset printed book jacket with saddle
sewn signatures
Papers: Finch Fine Digital 80 lb (cover),
Finch Fine Digital 80 lb (text), Curious Touch
80 lb (text)

Fonts: Adobe Clean, Adobe Minion Pro
Photographers: Phil Lu (cover photo),
Sam Wick, Shawn Cheris, Sonja Hernandez

Designer's Statement:

This little book is a primer for those who work
in or with XD, Adobe Experience Design, as
well as those who aspire to. It's a compilation of
beliefs, techniques, and motivations that give a
clear picture of the XD perspective on thinking
and making.

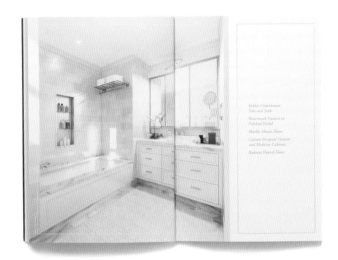

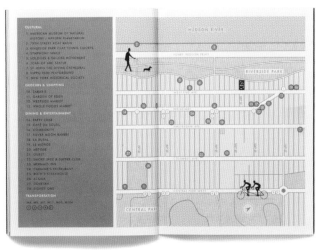

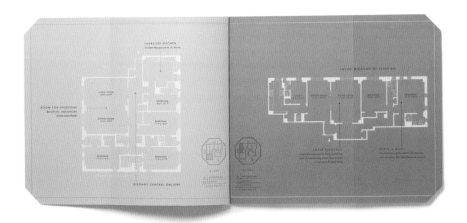

Title: 845 West End Avenue
Firm: And Partners NY
Creative Director: David Schimmel
Art Director: Craig Bailey
Designers: Craig Bailey, Antonio Mah
Client: Atlas Capital Group,
Sterling American Properties

Printer: Dynagraf Inc., Canton, MA
Method: Offset Embossed Metallic Foil cover,
perfect bound, die cut and gate folded pages
Papers: Neenah Paper, Eames Canvas,
110 lb (cover); Neenah Paper, Classic Crest,
80 lb (text)
Colors: 4 color + 2 PMS + metallic foil

Illustrator: Adam Simpson
Writer: Charlie Veprek

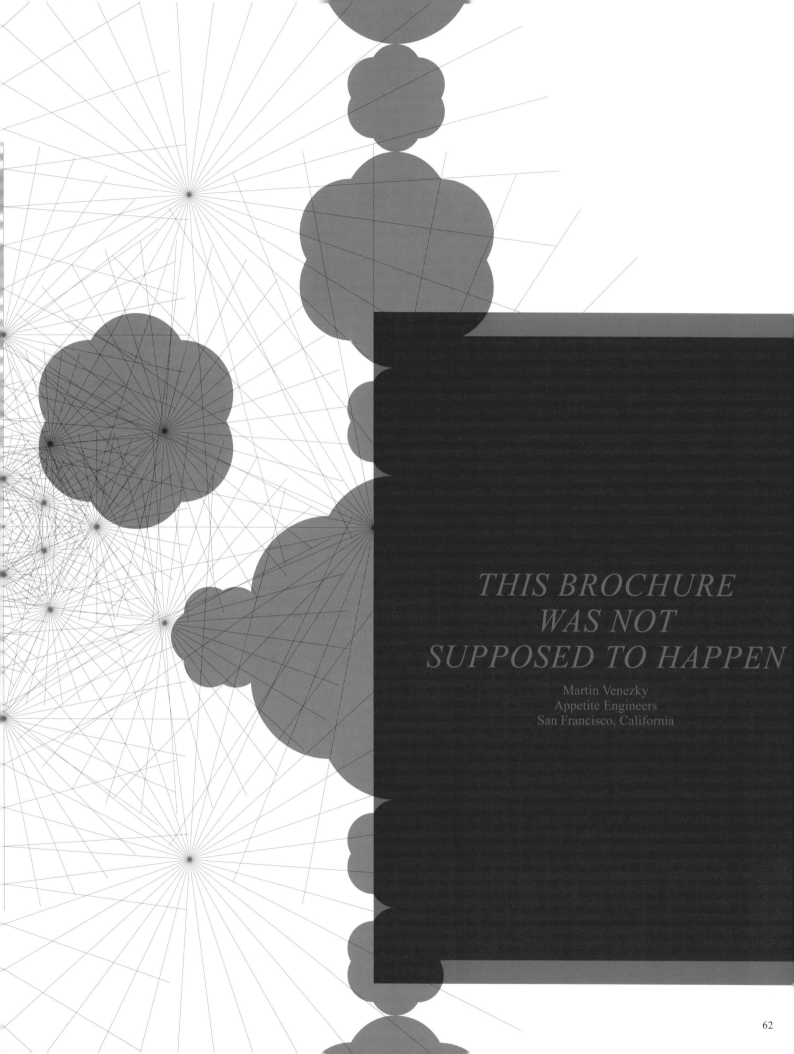

THIS BROCHURE WAS NOT SUPPOSED TO HAPPEN

Martin Venezky
Appetite Engineers
San Francisco, California

This brochure was not supposed to happen. Its creation was a subtle act of defiance and necessity, brought about by the California College of Art's newly minted policy that severely limited new printed materials. The communications department felt that eliminating print would send a positive message of environmental stewardship and concern. Perhaps it did. But it did other things, too.

Every year during the fall semester, graduate art programs gather for a series of portfolio events across the country. Direct engagement with serious potential candidates are valued moments. As prospects visited our table, their arms loaded with other schools' ambitious catalogs, this new initiative left us empty handed. We could only offer a flimsy postcard inviting them to read our documents online and a boilerplate booklet (created by the communications department) exhorting the fulfillment of graduate life in the most general terms possible. It was an embarrassing exercise.

There is a deeper meaning in the presentation and exchange of real materials: ceremony, gratitude, respect. When you are on the road meeting candidates, or in the classroom teaching those who have been admitted, you understand just how much these folks are putting on the line. A return to school is an enormous threshold to cross: redefining one's career, sharply bending one's trajectory, relinquishing predictability for an uncertain path. So something as simple as a brochure can make a difference at a vulnerable moment.

Moments like these, when the gesture and exchange have an inherent reassuring meaning, cannot be replicated through online media. But within an institution, the argument can be futile. That's why our core faculty decided that actually creating our own brochure, even in secret, was more important than arguing the benefits of print over digital.

We knew that if we were going to exercise defiance, the result had better be special. And if we were going to put up our own department funds and donate our own time and effort, we had better say something of significance, and craft an object of value and meaning—a showpiece for ourselves and the school.

So we tried to imagine what would please us. What would we want to receive and keep and examine and admire? Isn't this one of the great pleasures in design? When you can set aside messaging and demographics and budget and timetables, and just for a little while imagine saying something honestly—from one adult to another—about a subject that means a lot, and to realize that voice in an object of permanence and commitment.

We imagined topics of concern and controversy and how a poetic voice might mingle with a critical one. The text was written alongside the design, and the process helped generate the content. What are we concerned about as educators? As inhabitants of an urban world? We didn't need to be clever or sporty or smug. We examined pictures not of beaming students looking creative and scholarly, or lecturers looking concerned and wise, but my own personal shots of the designed world around us in all its complications and surprise.

Put aside was any notion of being the hippest on the block and instead we looked to old 19th-century postcards, and geometric structures: these are things we have all enjoyed as curious, collecting humans. We engineered the typographic details, small asides and footnotes, details within details; lists of things that fascinate us hidden behind back covers. The making of the brochure became its own continual discovery and led to lively conversation and debate.

I mentioned permanence and commitment. These words have critical value in today's online world. You can add slowness to that, too, for with this brochure, we were trying hard to reduce its speed of transmission. We wanted to make the most of our print resources to allow the public to mull over the issues and images and connections. It is very hard to mull over anything online.

Perhaps this is a lesson for those who consider everything print passé. Understand the medium for its special value. Put in the effort to make everything you print meaningful and worth the investment—no more clichés or wasted words. Save those for the Internet.

Martin

We love the visual layers—collages and textures from imagery and typography. The narrative is layered as well, it questions and posits, engages and challenges its audience—inspirational for a potential design graduate student, for us all.

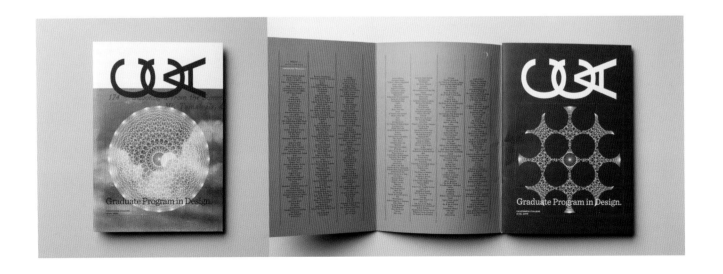

Title: CCA Graduate Program in Design
Firm: Appetite Engineers
Art Director: Martin Venezky
Designer: Martin Venezky
Client: California College of the Arts: Graduate
Program in Design
Client Industry: Education/Academia

Printer: Printcrafters, Winnipeg
Method: Offset
Paper: Cougar Vellum (text and cover)
Color: 4 color

Fonts: Sentinel, Avenir
Photographers: Martin Venezky, primary;
various others for student shots
Writers: Martin Venezky, Leslie Roberts,
Barry Katz

There is a luscious density in this piece as
well as an extraordinary attention to detail.
The mix of old and new images and layering
of line art framing give it a nostalgic yet
fresh quality.

Title: CCA Graduate Program in Design
Firm: Appetite Engineers

A collage of San Francisco transportation
infrastructure and annotations expresses
a context for the graduate program,
a physicality as well as a head space.

A collage of San Francsico architectural elements visually demonstrates the graduate program process and curriculum.

DESIGN
LEADERSHIP

THESIS

C R A F T

C O L L A B O R A T I O N

FORM
METHOD
PROCESS
MATERIALS

Form Studio
Topic Studios
Skill Studios
Electives

CRITICALITY

STRATEGIC THINKING
TRANS-DISCIPLINARITY
DESIGN DIRECTION
ENTREPRENEURSHIP

Thesis Research
Design Research
Group Projects
External Projects

CRITICAL THINKING
THEORY ● HISTORY
OBSERVATION

Design Writing
Design History
Seminars
Electives

DESIGN
RESEARCH

Title: SWA/Landscape Architecture, Planning,
Urban Design
Firm: Aufuldish & Warinner
Designer: Bob Aufuldish
Client: SWA Group
Client Industry: Landscape Architecture

Printer: Oscar Printing
Method: Offset
Colors: 4 color + metallic silver

Font: Myriad by Robert Slimbach and Carol
Twombly
Photographers: Tom Fox, Bill Tatham
Editor: Scott Cooper

Designer's Statement:
This brochure gives an overview of SWA's
areas of practice and shows a vast range of the
company's work. The grid developed for this
brochure is used to generate projects sheets
and other materials for SWA.

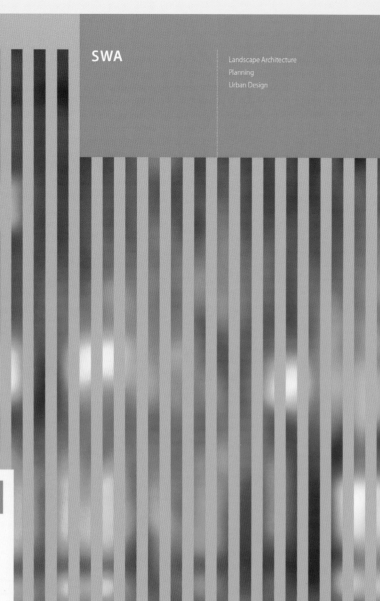

Title: A+E Field Guide
Firm: Brad Bartlett Design, Los Angeles
Art Director: Brad Bartlett
Designers: Brad Bartlett, Elaine Suh Bartlett
Client: Nevada Museum of Art
Client Industry: Arts/Culture

Printer: Clearimage Printing Company
Method: Offset
Paper: Sappi McCoy
Color: 6 color

Designer's Statement:

The *A+E Field Guide* was designed to accompany the 2011 Art + Environment Conference hosted by the Nevada Museum of Art. The booklet presents a series of provocations that encourage attendees to have a dialogue with the presenters by using QR codes for real-time feedback. Graphic elements were drawn from geothermal energy maps of the northern Nevada region.

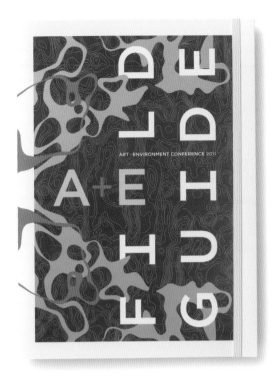

The Art + Environment Conference at the Nevada Museum of Art reaches across continents, disciplines, and media to unite a dynamic group of thinkers shaping ideas about human interactions with global environments. A flagship program of the Museum's Center for Art + Environment, the 2011 Conference brings together artists, scholars, designers, and writers for a dialogue that fosters new knowledge in the visual arts. The Museum's galleries feature exhibitions that explore our relationships with natural, built, and virtual environments, while serving as a springboard for Conference sessions and keynote presentations.

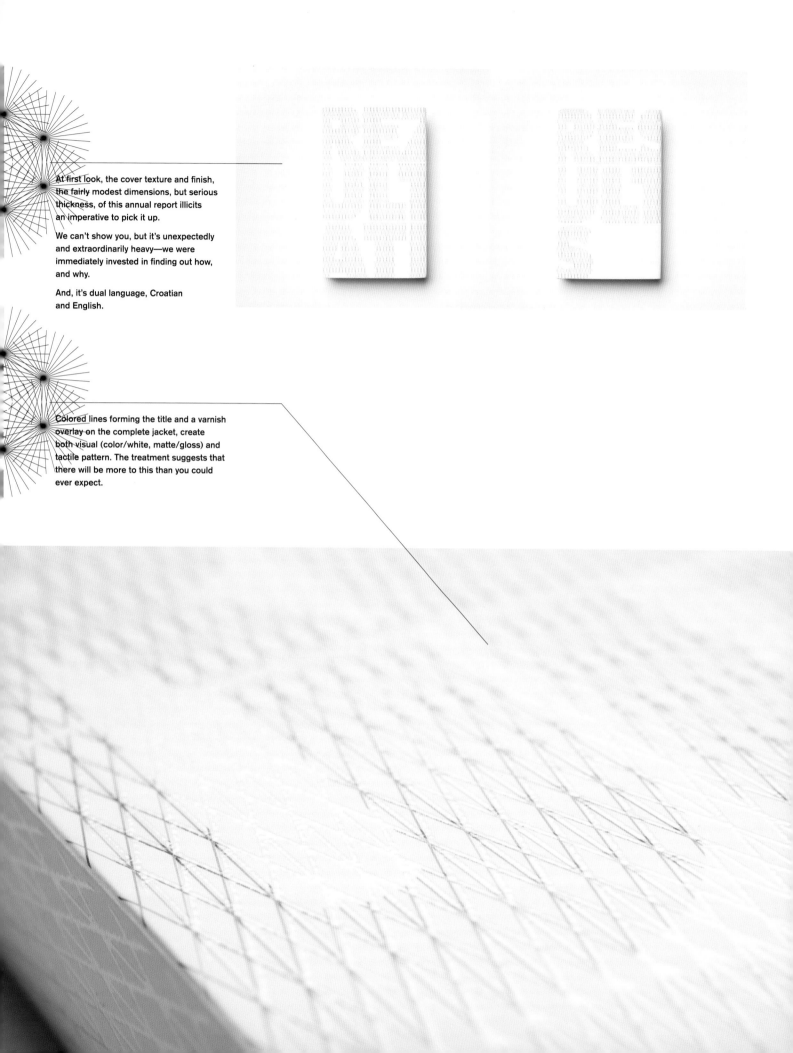

At first look, the cover texture and finish, the fairly modest dimensions, but serious thickness, of this annual report illicits an imperative to pick it up.

We can't show you, but it's unexpectedly and extraordinarily heavy—we were immediately invested in finding out how, and why.

And, it's dual language, Croatian and English.

Colored lines forming the title and a varnish overlay on the complete jacket, create both visual (color/white, matte/gloss) and tactile pattern. The treatment suggests that there will be more to this than you could ever expect.

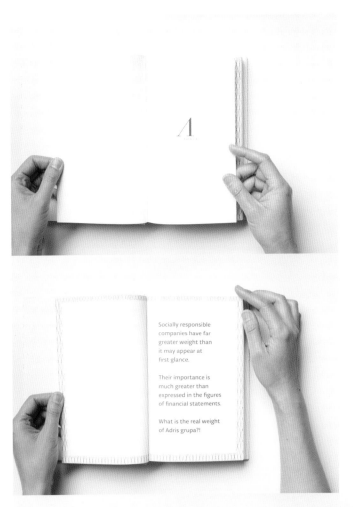

Title: Results 2010
Firm: Bruketa & Žinić OM
Art Directors: Davor Bruketa, Nikola Žinić
(Creative Directors); Nebojša Cvetkovi (Art
Director, Illustrator, Designer)
Designer: Nebojša Cvetkovi
Other Credits: Ivan Čadež (Senior Copywriter,
video editing), Ivanka Mabi (Account Director),
Martina Ivki (Account Executive), Vesna Đurašin
(Production Manager), Radovan Radievi (DTP)
Client: Adris Group
Client Industry: Investment

Printer: Cerovski Print Boutique
Methods: Foil stamping, Braille varnish

Fonts: TyponineSansPro, Minion Pro
Illustrator: Nebojša Cvetkovi
Writers: Ivan Čadež

Designer's Statement:

Investment company Adris group is a socially
responsible company. Its significance and
weight are much greater than what is expressed
in dull, dry financial statements.

That's why this year's Adris group annual
report, named simply *Results*, poses a question: What is the real weight of Adris group?
And then, despite being regular in size,
it answers the question by being very, very
heavy. The unexpected weight of the book
invites the reader to consider the true weight
of Adris Group.

**The pacing of full text pages, case studies,
and financials, aid the consumption of
information density.**

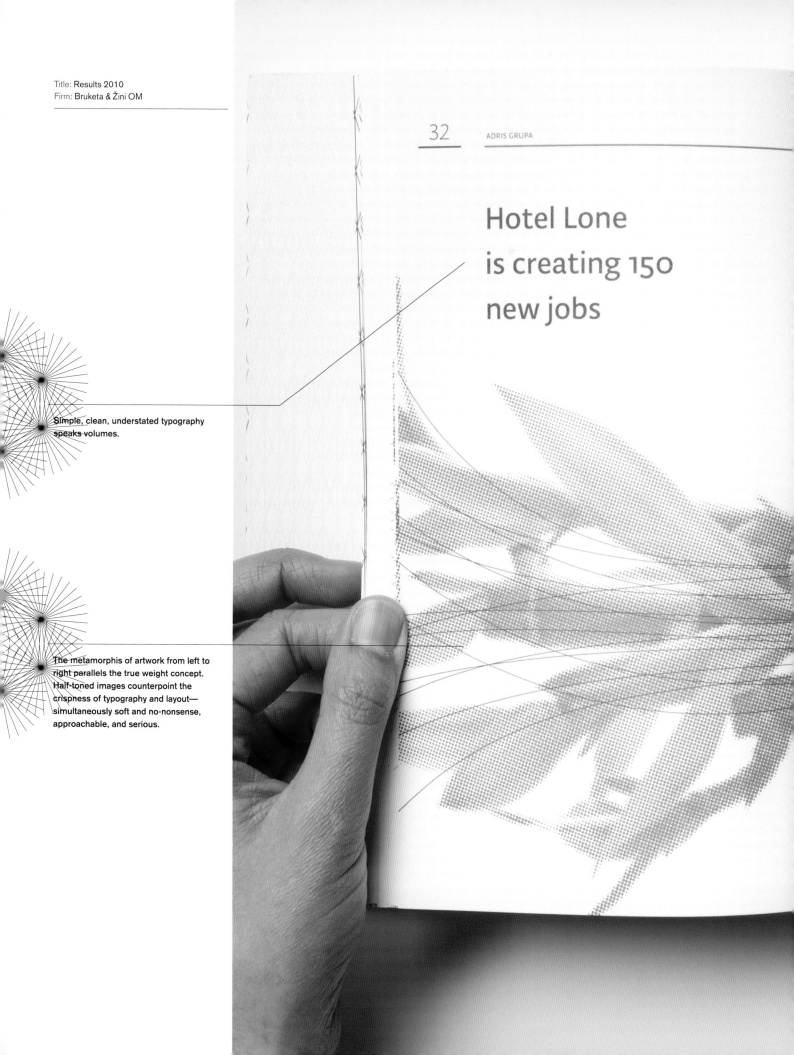

Title: Results 2010
Firm: Bruketa & Žini OM

Hotel Lone
is creating 150
new jobs

Simple, clean, understated typography speaks volumes.

The metamorphis of artwork from left to right parallels the true weight concept. Half-toned images counterpoint the crispness of typography and layout— simultaneously soft and no-nonsense, approachable, and serious.

OTEL LONE IS A
NOWROOM OF THE
ROATIAN CREATIVE
DUSTRY that has offered
ung architects, designers
d artists the opportunity
create a unique Croatian
oduct and to achieve
irmation and recognition
th in the region and in
e world, supporting faith
our own capabilities.

THIS IS
THE REAL WEIGHT
OF ADRIS GRUPA.

What Adris Group does is more than
the sum of it's parts, more than appearance.

The actual weight of the book reflects the
"real weight of Adris Group" concept—more
than the immediate numbers or statements
of facts, the company is defined by the
ultimate ramificatitons and impacts of its
policies and initiatives.

This self-mailer promo folds down like a road map and opens up into a poster. The back side is dense, full of small images of thirty projects with short descriptions. A lot to take in all at once, but it shows the depth and breadth of CCRZ's work.

Title: CCRZ promo
Firm: CCRZ
Art Director: Eugenio Castiglioni
Designer: Paolo Cavalli
Client: Studio CCRZ

Printer: Tecnografica
Method: Offset

Photographer: Eugenio Castiglioni

While the backside provides a bibliography of work, the front gives us context. We love how CCRZ has laid out all its pieces on the table and shot an overview.

The text works with the folds of the paper. The small type creates another layer of interest by use of scale contrast.

Uncoated paper brings an elegance that coated paper could never provide.

Title: **La Via Lattea**
Firm: **CCRZ**
Art Director: **Marco Zürcher**
Designer: **Marco Zürcher**
Client: **Teatro del Tempo**

Printers: **La Buona Stampa, Saica (box)**
Method: **Offset**

Artlog: Lida Baday/Spring 2010
Firm: Concrete Design Communications
Art Directors: Diti Katona, John Pylypczak
Designer: Melatan Riden
Client: Lida Baday
Client Industry: Fashion

Printer: Transcontinental PLM
Method: Offset
Color: 4 color

Photographer: Chris Nicholls

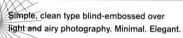

Simple, clean type blind-embossed over light and airy photography. Minimal. Elegant.

Title: Lida Baday/Fall/Winter 2010
Firm: Concrete Design Communications
Art Director: Diti Katona/John Pylypczak
Designer: Melatan Riden
Client: Lida Baday
Client Industry: Fashion

Printer: Transcontinental PLM
Method: Offset
Colors: 4 color + 1 foil

Photographer: Chris Nicholls

Designer's Statement:

With offices in Toronto and New York, Lida Baday designs and produces well-detailed, beautiful clothing that captures the essence of thoughtful, discerning, and modern women. Her collections are sold in luxury boutiques and retailers around the world including Saks Fifth Avenue. The designer does virtually no advertising, so the brochure acts as the company's only promotional vehicle.

These brochures are the latest in a series that Concrete has developed for the fashion designer over a fifteen year relationship. The visual language of the brand employs sensual, timeless photography as a signature style. A combination of different paper stocks, printing techniques, distinctive photographic techniques, and cropping all allude to the designer's hallmark of impeccable detailed clothing.

High-gloss foil stamp on the cover makes the white type on white background pop.

A combination of uncoated and coated paper in the interior adds a layer of texture. Odd super–imposed imagery on the model adds another visual layer and takes the piece to higher level beyond a typical fashion brochure.

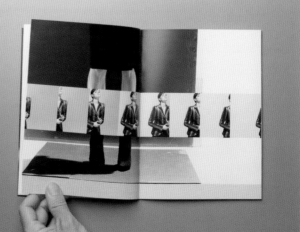

Simple, clean, understated photography with unexpected foldouts. There is no text at all inside the brochure. The images speak for themselves.

Title: Lida Baday/Spring 2011
Firm: Concrete Design Communications
Art Director: Diti Katona, John Pylypczak
Designer: Melatan Riden
Client: Lida Baday
Client Industry: Fashion

Printer: Transcontinental PLM
Method: Offset
Color: 4 color + 1 foil

Photographer: Chris Nicholls

Ultra-thin type is foil stamped in silver so it changes appearance as you move the brochure.

Unusual cropping and orientation highlights the experience of fashion as art.

Title: A New Angle
Firm: Design Army
Art Directors: Pum Lefebure, Jake Lefebure
Designer: Mariela Hsu
Client: Golden Triangle BID
Client Industry: Real Estate Development

Printer: Westland Enterprises
Method: Offset
Colors: 2 PMS + gold foil

Writer: Jasmine Probst

Designer's Statement:

Created to attract a higer-end retailer to a more business–oriented part of the city, it's loud and pink—just the way fashion-forward retailers like it. Additionally, we have a unique folded angle cover to reinforce our title, "A New Angle," and it's a subtle nod to the organizations name (Golden Triangle).

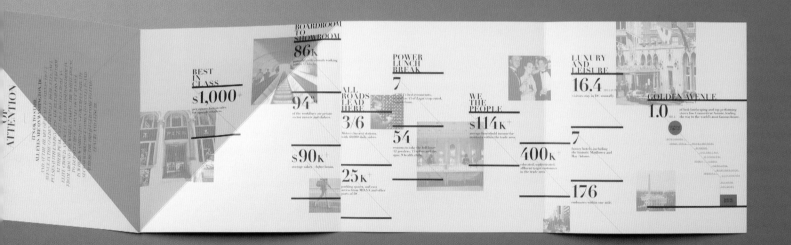

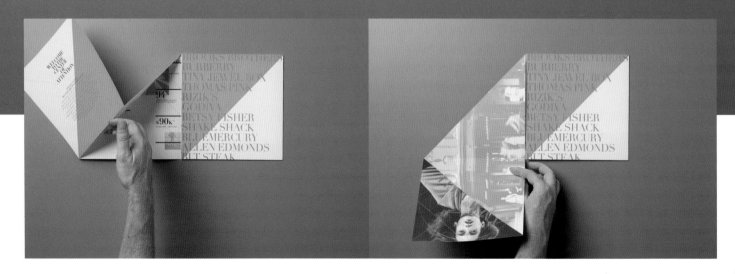

Title: the spot for luxury living
Firm: Design Army
Art Directors: Pum Lefebure, Jake Lefebure
Designers: Mariela Hsu, Sucha Becky
Client: JBG Companies
Client Industry: Real Estate Development

Printer: Westland Enterprises
Method: HP Indigo/Digital
Color: 4-color process

Writer: Jasmine Probst

Designer's Statement:

Promotional event brochure to announce a
new project (Louis at 14) in the heart of the
14th/U Street area in Washington DC. The
name of the building is referenced to Loius the
14th and Louis (Oppulance, Decadence, and
Dignified) and Louis Armstrong (Jazz and Ust
area legend).

Artlog: Moving Ahead/KCMO CDE FY 2011
Annual Report
Firm: Design Ranch
Client: KCMO CDE
Client Industry: Nonprofit

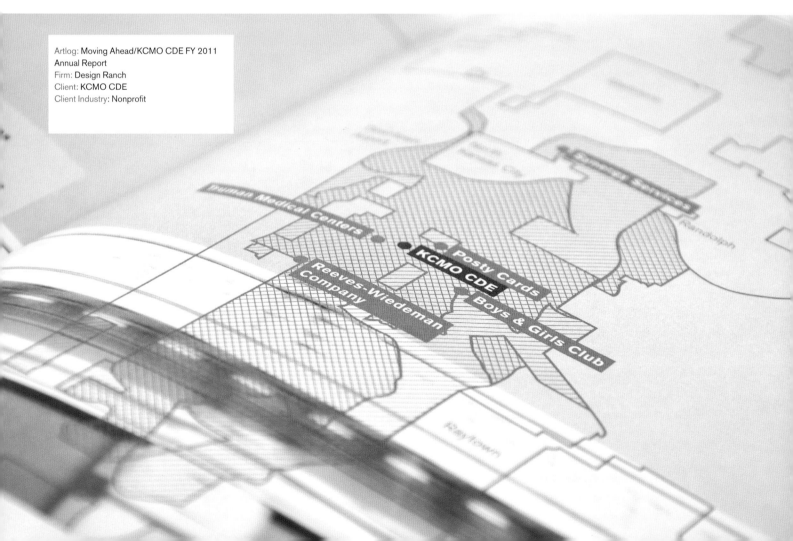

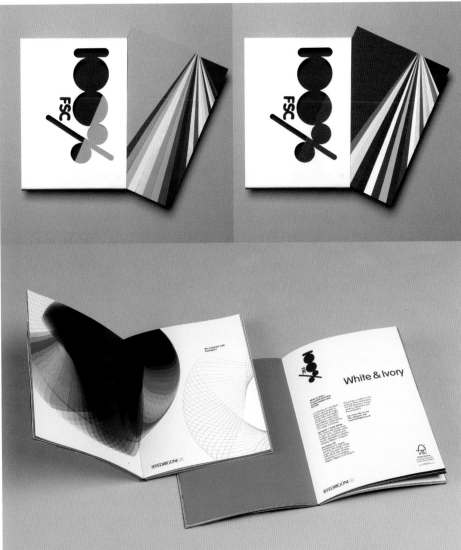

Title: 100% FSC/Fedrigoni
Firm: Design LSC
Designer: Luigi Carnovale
Client: Fedrigoni UK
Client Industry: Fedrigoni is a manufacturer of high-quality Italian papers and boards for designers and printers, distributed to over 80 countries.

Printer: NB Colour Printers
Paper: Fedrigoni FSC papers, each individually die cut, foiled embossed and printed
Method: Litho
Colors: 4 color + PMS 877 metallic with Inline gloss and matte spot varnish

Fonts: Special designed Font 'One'00', VAG Rounded

Designer's Statement:

A series of four limited–edition books for the new Fedrigoni Collection of FSC papers and boards, each book references one of four elements—earth, water, air, and fire—each inspired by the many different textures and colors available in this imaginative range. Through a combination of color and texture, print and finish, each book presents a selection of the very special and unique papers available from the Fedrigoni FSC range.

These books are not only practical when looking for a paper with environmental credentials, but integrate practicality with plain and printed samples of the selected papers.

Title: Vintage by Hemingway Design/Graham
& Brown
Firm: Design LSC
Designer: Luigi Carnovale
Client: Graham & Brown
Client Industry: Graham & Brown is a British
designer and manufacturer of high quality
Wall Coverings. Their designs cover domestic
walls the world over.

Printer: Team Impression, Leeds UK
Papers: 85 gsm, 100 gsm, and 300 gsm
Fedrigoni Arcoprint Milk
Method: Litho
Color: 4 color

Fonts: Futura. All other fonts were drawn or
modified specifically.
Photographer: Lime

Designer's Statement:

A promotional pack designed to promote the
launch of four brand new wallpaper designs.
A collection of wallpapers, designed as part
of the Hemingway's award-winning Vintage
Festival, and hosted at London's Southbank
Centre. Each design pays tribute to the Festival
of Britain's 60th anniversary—the same
year Graham & Brown celebrates its 65th
anniversary—the collection is a homage to
Britain's design heritage. The pack includes
four booklets, each taking its inspiration from a
different decade: "Deco Diamond" celebrates
the glittering 1930s; with distinct graphic
influences; "Grid" is Mad Men '50s chic;
"Loopy Lines" heralds the free-flowing style
of the 1960s; and "Do the Stretch" captures
'70s glam rock with a hint of *Space Odyssey*.
The pack was used to launch the wallpaper
collection at the Vintage Festival, and later
mailed to editors of leading fashion and interior
magazines throughout the world.

**The folder provides a holder for the interior
brochure. Once unfolded, a substantial real
swatch of wallpaper is revealed showing the
pattern at full size.**

Deco
Diamond

BY
HEMINGWAY
DESIGN

INSPIRED BY 1930s GLAMOUR,
THIS ART DECO PATTERN TAKES ITS
CUE FROM THE DECADE'S EMERALD
ONYX ORNAMENTS, ENAMEL
KITCHENWARE AND
WAYNE'S COLLECTION OF
78 RECORD COVERS

GRAHAM & BROWN

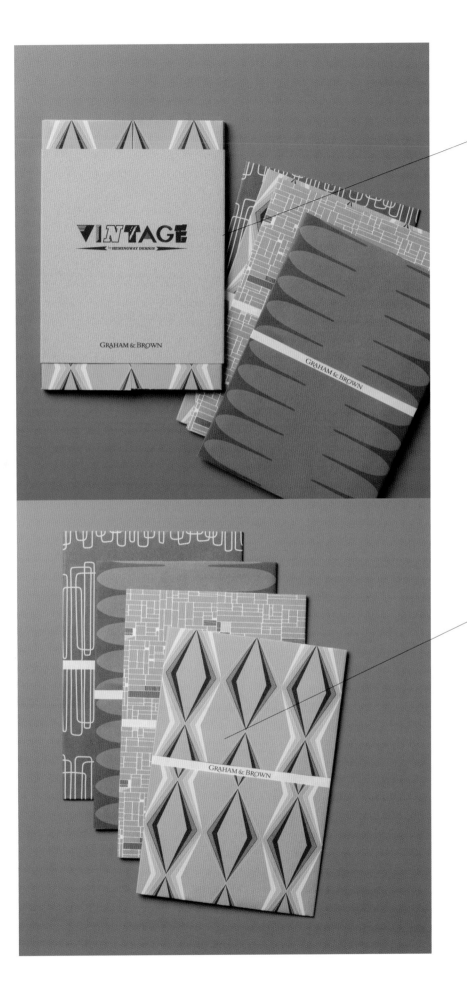

A belly band keeps a series of four swatches intact.

An interesting foldover allows the company logo to appear on the front side of the piece when it is actually printed on the back.

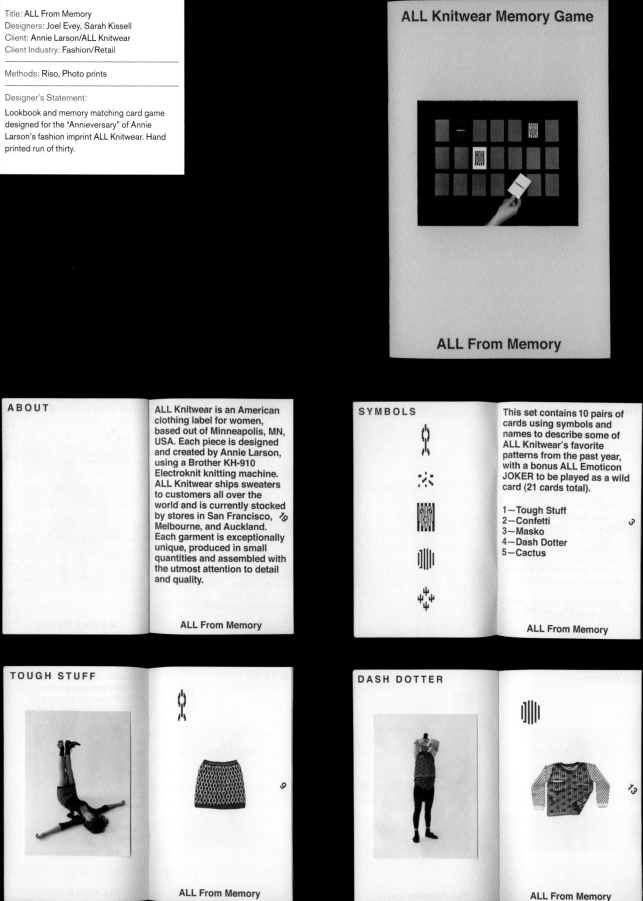

ALL Knitwear Memory Game

ALL From Memory

ABOUT

ALL Knitwear is an American clothing label for women, based out of Minneapolis, MN, USA. Each piece is designed and created by Annie Larson, using a Brother KH-910 Electroknit knitting machine. ALL Knitwear ships sweaters to customers all over the world and is currently stocked by stores in San Francisco, Melbourne, and Auckland. Each garment is exceptionally unique, produced in small quantities and assembled with the utmost attention to detail and quality.

ALL From Memory

SYMBOLS

This set contains 10 pairs of cards using symbols and names to describe some of ALL Knitwear's favorite patterns from the past year, with a bonus ALL Emoticon JOKER to be played as a wild card (21 cards total).

1—Tough Stuff
2—Confetti
3—Masko
4—Dash Dotter
5—Cactus

ALL From Memory

TOUGH STUFF

ALL From Memory

DASH DOTTER

ALL From Memory

W T V R

The International Issue

Title: W T V R
Firm: Urban Outfitters
Art Directors: Joel Evey, Matt Owen
Designer: Namik Schwarz
Client: Urban Outfitters
Client Industry: Fashion/Retail

Color: 1 color

Designer's Statement:
W T V R is a zine published by Urban Outfitters to promote music and cultural content from Urban's blog in the stores. It features interviews with artists, musicians, and photographers such as Toro Y Moi and Tim Barber.

About an Aussie Girl

Our blog correspondent Nadia Saccardo schools us on everything cool down under.

In a sentence, how would you describe Australia to someone in the U.S.? Very, very far away, but surprisingly similar to parts of the U.S. Especially the West Coast.

Where are your favorite places in Australia to: Dance like a crazy person? In Sydney, Goodgod Small Club, the later the better. In Melbourne, the Bamboo Musik parties make the best dance. If I'm not there, I will be at K Box Karaoke making the worst dance.

Shop for a cute dress? Go to Via Alley for interesting international labels and cuter-than-kittens homeware from Japan. Sydney also has more vintage markets than you could point a lace-up boot at.

Listen to some live music? Manning Bar is in the middle of Sydney University, which (depending on your age) will make you feel much younger or much older than you probably are. I'm riddled with Peter Pan syndrome so I love it but, word of warning, check what's on there before you go. Waves—good. Seekae—good. Battle of the Bands—bad. Goodgod Small Club consistently plays fun music, until very late, in its "dancetería" out back. In Melbourne, The Forum if the talent is good, but a safer bet is The Toff

In Town, which consistently pulls in top bands and DJs.

Enjoy the great outdoors? For some miraculous reason, there are parts of Sydney Harbour that you can still swim in. Away from the water, please try and see the Wendy Whiteley Garden at Lavender Bay and the Rose Seidler House at Wahroonga. Melbourne used to be called 'The Garden State' for a reason. Go with the flow and sit in a park like the Fitzroy Gardens, the Botanic Gardens or the Flagstaff Gardens (anything with an official "garden" on the end should do it). Take a book and a bottle of wine with you too—it's very Melbourne.

What's the best way to spend a day in Sydney? I'll keep this short and to the point: Breakfast in Bondi at Jed's or Porch & Parlour—make sure to drink at least two flat whites. Then go jump off the North Bondi rocks. Bus or cab towards the city past Ariel Books on Oxford Street and duck into Aesop for some nice smelling beauty things. Stop for a second swim at Andrew Boy Charlton in Woolloomooloo and have a coffee there, too. Walk up Bourke Street past Sable & Argent bike shop. Grab a negroni at Love Tilly Devine then head to Centennial Park for a pre-dinner nap by the duck pond. Eat for hours at Eathouse Diner and stay for dessert. Dance like an idiot at Goodgod.

Closet Project

How globe-trotting model Anastasia Krivosheeva fills her suitcase

Name: Anastasia Krivosheeva

Hometown: Moscow

What was the last place you traveled for work: New York

For fun: Saint Tropez

What's your favorite plane movie? Depends on the mood, it's good to watch some "easy" movies on the plane, like comedies or I also love to watch old movies.

What's your favorite airport? I think it's Sheremetyevo in Moscow. It's super old, but it feels so sweet, when you step off the plane and you have in mind that you're almost home.

What piece of clothing do you take on every trip? I have one jacket made from green leather. I bought it like five years ago or something, but it's still one of my favorites. Once I forgot it in Moscow! I always have a lot of stuff with me, but always feel like I don't have anything to wear!

What are your travel essentials? iPhone; hygiene stuff; jeans with sneakers; small black dress with heels; passport!

What is the best souvenir that you've ever brought home from a trip? I collect coins from all the countries, I'm trying to get the old ones from all too!

The stupidest souvenir? Postcards

What's your favorite part of travel? Seeing different cultures.

What's the next new place you want to visit? I want to go to India one day.

Mala-baba

Accessories designer Ana Carrasco finds Madrid heavenly

Name: Ana Carrasco

Hometown: Madrid, Spain

How would you describe your city in one sentence? The most active city in the world.

Who is the most famous person in your city? This is the capital of Spain—80 percent of the famous Spanish people live here, from the Royal Family to all of the government and most of the artists. Perhaps the most famous are Penelope Cruz and Javier Bardem—they used to live here before moving to L.A.

What's the most amazing thing you've ever seen there? During August at lunch time, I've seen one of the major streets without anybody, no cars or people, just really empty. Just once and for a few minutes.

If you could rewrite your city's slogan, what would it say? The actual one is "From Madrid to Heaven." I won't change it.

If you were forced out of Madrid, where would you move and why? To the countryside, looking for nature and peace.

What's the biggest fashion trend right now? That's the good thing about Madrid, you can see a lot of different people and a lot of trends. People are free to wear what they want. When I travel, I realize that in most of the big cities, everybody wears similar trends.

If you could rewrite your city's slogan, what would it say? The actual one is "From Madrid to Heaven." I

What's a phrase all the locals use? Se sale! It's similar to "cool."

How does where you live influence your designs? In Spain we have incredible light during the year and that makes me unafraid to use all the colors.

What are you most proud of about where you're from? The people—you can always find people laughing. It's a happy city, we love going out and having a beer and we are open to new people and cultures.

Stolen Girlfriends Club

Sexy clothes designed by a trio of Kiwi surfers.

Name: Luke Harwood

Hometown: Auckland, New Zealand

everyone... you can't walk down the street without seeing someone you know!

Who is the most famous person from your city? A famous old band called Crowded House... Liam Finn is killing it on an International stage. Ladyhawke has been doing well music wise. Then there's Rhys Darby, aka Murray from Flight of the Concords. And Taika Waititi, director of the film Boy and leader of the Crazy Horses, is one clever man!

If you were forced out of Auckland, where would you move? New York is a lot of fun, we could definitely live there!

What's the biggest fashion trend in Auckland right now? Leather, denim and more leather... you could say "Hell for Leather."

What's some slang that all the locals use? Brother, bro, yeah man!

What are you most proud of about Auckland? In New Zealand everyone is

How would you describe your city in one sentence? Everyone knows

If you could rewrite your city's slogan, what would it say? The City of Pirates!

low key... they don't care much for fame or status, they care more about their work!

1

Designed by Serl Brij

4

2

3

Title: Singing Beach
Art Director: Joel Evey
Client: Colin Leaman
Client Industry: Photography

Printer: Linco
Method: Web Press
Paper: 50 lb Bond
Color: 1 color

Designer's Statement:

Folding publication of photographs by
Colin Leaman

ALICIA

ALICIA
Alimentación y Ciencia
Naming de una Fundación Gastronómica
NOM-NAM para Cla-se

NUAT

NUAT, Vino blanco
Naming para cla-se

Premio Laus 2010
Categoria de naming

The strength of this collection of cards comes from each card having a different process associated with the simple word on the front.

This card is printed on a soft suede, flocked paper that enhances the warmth and works well with "Mama."

MAMA

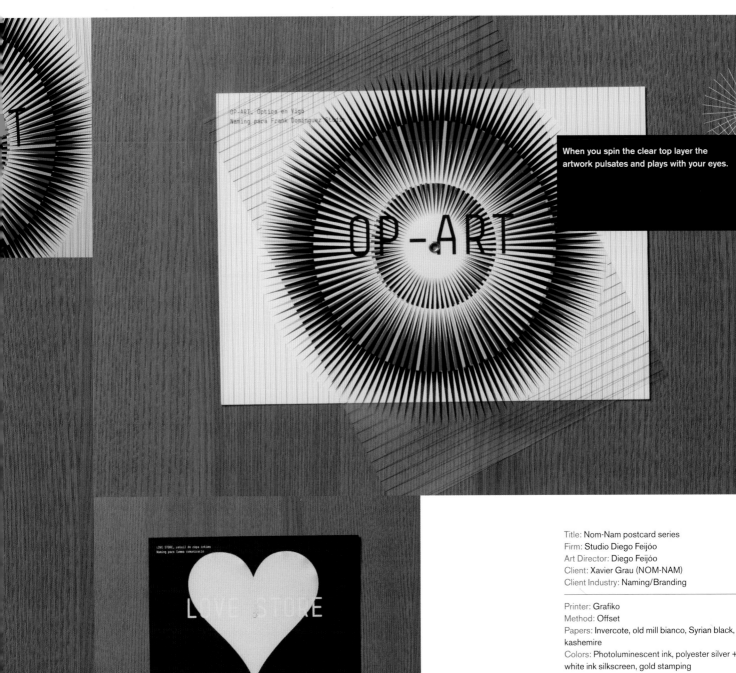

When you spin the clear top layer the artwork pulsates and plays with your eyes.

OP-ART

OP-ART, Optica en Vigo
Naming para Frank Dominguez

LOVE STORE, retail de ropa íntima
Naming para Somos comunicació

LOVE STORE

Title: Nom-Nam postcard series
Firm: Studio Diego Feijóo
Art Director: Diego Feijóo
Client: Xavier Grau (NOM-NAM)
Client Industry: Naming/Branding

Printer: Grafiko
Method: Offset
Papers: Invercote, old mill bianco, Syrian black, kashemire
Colors: Photoluminescent ink, polyester silver + white ink silkscreen, gold stamping

Font: "Simple" font

Designer's Statement:

Naming agency promotional postcards. Each postcard illustrates the meaning of a name created by NOM-NAM. All names are set with the same font, and on the same size and position, using selected printing specifications on each one to illustrate the meaning of each promoted name.

1. ALICIA : Alice Through the Looking Glass (Name for a Science Foundation)
2. OP-ART: Optical game (Name for an optical retail)
3. NUAT: In Heraldic, Lion tail (Name for a wine)
4. LOVESTORE: Name for Lingerie Retail
5. MAMA: Name for Maternal milk bank

Title: Premis Delta '11
Firm: Studio Diego Feijóo
Art Director: Diego Feijóo
Client: Delta Awards/ADI-FAD Spain
Client Industry: Product/Manufacturing

Method: Offset
Paper: Cromolux paper
Color: 4 color

Font: Helvetica

Designer's Statement:

Call for entries brochure for a competition for best product design, illustrated using equilateral triangles (Delta)

Title: Elfen promo
Firm: Elfen
Photographer: Mike Chapman, Guto Evans,
Christing Glade, Jelani Memory,
Warren Orchard, Huw Talfryn, Pete Teifer

Method: Offset
Paper: Cyclus offset
Color: CMYK
Fonts: Vag Rounded, Univers

Designer's Statement:

Self promotion piece for the Elfen studio,
celebrating 10 years in business. It is a docu-
mentation of things that we had collected over
a decade laid out on our ping pong table, with a
reference to the start date….

Title: ACAD Annual Report
Firm: Foundry Communications
Art Director: Zahra Al-Harazi
Designer: Jake Lim
Client: Alberta College of Art and Design
(ACAD)

Printer: Blanchette Press

Photographer: Fritz Tolentino
Writer: Mel Woyituk

Designer's Statement:

The 2011 annual report showcases the unique
and important role ACAD plays within the
cultural and educational fabric of the Province.
ACAD is a catalyst institution. It is a place of
creative excellence where students emerge
as creative thinkers and innovative problem
solvers. The elastic bands that wrap around
the annual report symbolize the community
affiliated with ACAD who are all bound together
with the same vision for ACAD, while also
tuning their individual voices. To supplement
the annual report, we created a booklet that
challenged over fifty ways to use elastic bands.
The purpose was to encourage people to
find their inner creative by taking something ordinarily mundane and finding ways
to make it interesting.

Title: Savanna Energy 10th Anniversary Annual Report
Firm: Foundry Communications
Art Director: Zahra Al-Harazi
Designers: Kylie Henry, Jake Lim, Andrea Merkl
Client: Energy

Printer: Blanchette Press

Writer: Jenny Allford

Designer's Statement:

Because this was Savanna's 10th year in business, this annual had to tell the story of not just the year in review but also the decade. The annual was split into two books: the first book is a marketing piece that conveys Savanna's objectives, and the second book contains the MD&A and financials. The first book is split into ten chapters; each chapter communicated one of Savanna's strengths and has a different visual aesthetic. The purpose of having each chapter be different was to reflect the diverse backgrounds and multifaceted nature to Savanna's business.

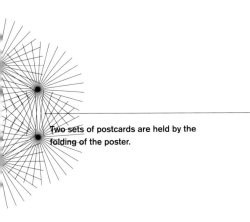

Two sets of postcards are held by the folding of the poster.

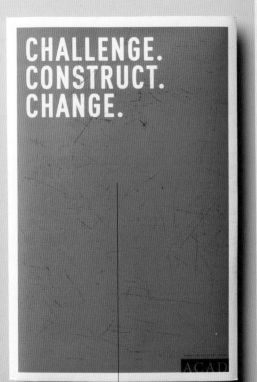

CHALLENGE.
CONSTRUCT.
CHANGE.

ACAD

DISCOVER ACAD
acad.ca

CHAT WITH ACAD
(403) 284 7600
insp@acad.ca

VISIT ACAD
Alberta College of Art + Design
1407-14 Ave NW
Calgary, Alberta, Canada
T2N 4R3

BUILDING ACCESS
Monday - Friday
7:00 AM - 11:00 PM
Saturday, Sunday & Holidays
5:00 AM - 6:00 PM

BUSINESS HOURS
Weekdays
8:00 AM - 4:00 PM

FOLLOW ACAD
@ACADonline

LIKE ACAD
facebook.com/AlbertaCollege
ofArtandDesign

WATCH ACAD
youtube.com/ACADonline
vimeo.com/ACADonline

WELCOME
TO THE
ALBERTA
COLLEGE
OF ART +
DESIGN

ACAD

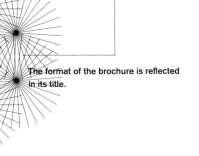

The format of the brochure is reflected in its title.

98

Title: ACAD Capital Package
Firm: Foundry Communications
Art Director: Zahra Al-Harazi
Designer: Jake Lim
Client: Alberta College of Art and Design
(ACAD)

Writer: Mel Woyituk

WHO WE ARE

ACAD students explore their passion for
creative thinking with an undergraduate degree
in Design or Fine Art.

With 11 unique programs including Photography,
Visual Communications Design, Ceramics,
Drawing, Fibre, Glass, Jewellery + Metals, Media
Arts + Digital Technologies, Painting, Print
Media and Sculpture, ACAD offers a rigorous
studio program which produces inventive
thinkers, visually acute learners and leading
problem solvers for today's creative economy.

ACAD is distinct in the way that it provides
undergraduate Bachelor of Fine Arts and Bachelor
of Design students a multidisciplinary curriculum
with the necessary freedom to develop as artists,
designers and creative thinkers. Our students
translate the most complex ideas into tangible
forms—paintings, glass work, sculpture, films,
performances, books, installations, inventions,
community projects and more often than not,
a combination of the above. Their time at ACAD
is focused on working one-on-one with practicing
artist and designer faculty to become powerful
creators and creative thinkers, able to discover
new and innovative ways of changing their fields
of endeavor, whatever these may be. Few
schools in Canada provide such a broad range
of possibilities.

ACAD has been the home of some of the most
exciting voices in contemporary art and design in
Canada for over 85 years. With a comprehensive
curriculum filled with a range of programs sure
to inspire, challenge and stimulate emerging
artists and designers, ACAD is the leading choice
for students who go on to work in a spectrum of
creative industries—doing what they love while

building impressive careers that impact the world
of art and design.

ACAD is a leading centre for education and
research, and a catalyst for creative inquiry and
cultural development. Located in Calgary and
overlooking the downtown core, ACAD provides a
unique undergraduate experience for students in
fine art, design and new media—an experience set
in the context of relevant, complementary liberal
studies and practical theory. Our Photography and
Visual Communications Design majors prepare
students for successful careers as professionals in
the discipline, practice and culture of photography
and design. And our Bachelor of Fine Arts program
is one of Canada's most prestigious studio-based
fine art programs.

What does an undergraduate degree at ACAD look
like? Our degree programs are studio-based, which
means hands-on. In our studios students explore
multiple media, applying new techniques and
immersing themselves in the practice and culture
of art and design. Students have access to a wide
range of unique opportunities, including a strong
international exchange program and a robust
scholarship and awards offering for incoming
students. Most importantly, with a 19 faculty-to-
student ratio, our average studio class is kept to 15
students ensuring that students receive individual,
personal attention from a faculty made up of a
diverse group of over 115 professional practicing
artists, designers and scholars.

This is a time of dynamic growth for ACAD.
As we continue to carve out an important
role as a leader in cultural development
and cultural research, we are expanding our
campus, our program offerings, our degree
streams, and our community activities.
We have adopted a new mandate and vision:
we have established our Institute for the

Creative Process (ICP@ACAD); and we have
led public discourse on imagination, arts
and community.

To show your support for the work done by the
Alberta College of Art + Design, please contact
our Office of Advancement at 403.284.7650, or
visit us at acad.ca/support.

REPEAT.

Every day we see opportunities
to affect the world around us.
As a creative catalyst, we want
to continue to inspire students
and our community but need the
support from the people who
believe in what we do.

WANT TO KNOW MORE?

Visit acad.ca for more info, or
book a tour to come see it for yourself at
acad.ca/tour. or rsvp@acad.ca.

S, SCULPTURE,
PRINT MEDIA, PAIN
, MEDIA ARTS + D
OGIES, JEWELLER
PHOTOGRAPHY, VM
CATIONS + DESIG

ACAD WAS FOUNDED IN

92

AVERAGE STUDIO

AND FEES

AND FEES

There is a rough quality to the treatment of
the typography and imagery that although
intricate, keeps the brochure from feeling
too precious.

Title: ACAD Capital Package
Firm: Foundry Communications

Once unfolded, a small piece becomes large—an unexpected and exciting development. A simple typeface contrasts the complex imagery.

WHY
RANSFORM?

a facility expansion, ACAD cannot
d develop new programs in keeping
Province's vision for success.

vision of new programming offerings for
creative students in areas such as moving
creative entrepreneurship and aboriginal
s dependent on new and improved space
tudents to learn and create.

t a facility expansion, ACAD cannot
nodate our anticipated growth in
population.

current facility is designed to
nodate nearly 400 fewer students than
lled at the College this year, and we
te continued growth in our future. Our
d long-term enrollment target of 1,500 Full
uivalent students is based on preliminary
concepts previously discussed with the
al Government and is estimated to be
d within a five year period. This goal is nearly
the capacity of ACAD's current facility.

t a facility expansion, ACAD cannot
ute to the innovative and
reneurial spirit of our Province.

dedicated to the creation of new
ions for our Province, and to continue
rations between Alberta's business and
communities. Through the Institute for
ative Process, we develop, research and
with leading businesses from across
untry to enhance our Province's future.
h the development of new space, ACAD

will be able to increase the reach of the ICP and
the work done currently.

Without a facility expansion, ACAD cannot
contribute to the creative culture of our
home, the City of Calgary.

Currently, Calgary lacks a major contemporary
art gallery — something ACAD is exploring as
a possibility in our proposed new facility. With
this in mind, our new expanded campus would
also offer gallery space for student exhibitions,
lecture theatres for visiting artists from around
the world, and community space for Calgary's
creative art and design culture.

Without a facility expansion, ACAD cannot
fully achieve the goal of offering unique
and in-demand Graduate programming for
students from around the world.

In 2013, ACAD is expecting to announce the
start of our first Masters level Graduate program
— a program that requires additional space and
support. With an overall target enrolment of
100 graduate students, there is a clear need for
additional studio and graduate seminar space to
ensure the success of ACAD's first Master of Fine
Arts in Craft Media program offering.

GET INVOLVED IN THE TRANSFORMATION

acad.ca/transformation

(403) 284 7600

1407–14 Ave NW
Calgary, Alberta, Canada
T2N 4R3

MK.
ARE.
ATE.

11 GREAT & UNIQUE PROGRAMS

CERAMICS, SCULPTURE, GLASS, PRINT MEDIA, PAIN
DRAWING, MEDIA ARTS + D
TECHNOLOGIES, JEWELLERY
METALS, PHOTOGRAPHY, VI
COMMUNICATIONS + DESIG
& FIBRE.

CAMPUS SIZE

27,000 m²

ACAD WAS FOUNDED IN

192

10 STUDENT GALLERIES ON CAMPUS **2** PROFESSIONAL GALLERIES ON CAMPUS

AVERAGE ACADEMIC CLASS SIZE   AVERAGE STUDIO

$ 5,191 DOMESTIC TUITION AND FEES (ONE YEAR, FULL TIME)

$ 14,815 INTERNATIONAL TUITION AND FEES (ONE YEAR, FULL TIME)

Title: Insight—Behind the scenes at the
London Vision Cliniic
Firm: hat-trick design
Art Directors: Jim Sutherland & Gareth Howat
Designers: Mark Wheatcroft & Gareth Howat
Client: London Vision Clinic
Client Industry: Medical

Printer: Boss Print
Method: Litho
Paper: Antalis McNaughton

Fonts: Bliss

It's about trust.
Your eyesight is one of
the most precious gifts
you possess. So who
can you trust to look
after it? That's the
fundamental question
for anyone considering
laser eye surgery.

Title: House of Illustration
Firm: hat-trick design
Art Directors: Jim Sutherland and
Gareth Howat
Designer: Alexandra Jurva
Client: House of Illustration
Client Industry: Non-profit

Printer: Pure print Group Limited
(Beacon Press)
Method: Digital
Paper: Naturalis Matt Absolute White

Fonts: Univers, ITC Lubalin Graph
Illustrators: Various

Designer's Statement:

The brainchild of Quentin Blake, The House
of Illustration will be the place to see past and
present illustration, both British and international. The Hous e of Illustration wants to put
illustration center stage and give it the attention
it deserves.

The identity would have to work with a wide
range of illustration styles.

Using a graphic sketchbook page as
a logotype, any style of illustration can be
incorporated, or it can be left blank,
as an inspiring space.

Miniature sketchbooks were used for business
cards, so that the recipients feel they are being
handed a page torn out from Quentin Blake's
sketchbook. The logo is also used as a publisher's mark on book spines.

Artlog: 091
Firm: hat-trick design
Art Directors: Jim Sutherland, Gareth Howat
Designer: Alex Swatridge
Client: British Heart Foundation
Client Industry: Non-profit/Philanthropy

Printer: Breckland Print
Method: Litho, Digital
Paper: Individual cards, placements, invitations,
booklet, sticker pad in maltese cross style box.
Mixture of paper stocks used but majority of the
pack was printed on Incada silk.

Fonts: Myriad
Photographer: John Ross
Illustrator: Rebecca Sutherland
Writers: Lizzie Harris (recipes), Nick Asbury
(games and guide)

The illustrations are clean and simple,
kid friendly and fun—very Japanese!
Patterns mixed will illustrations feel both
geometric and organic.

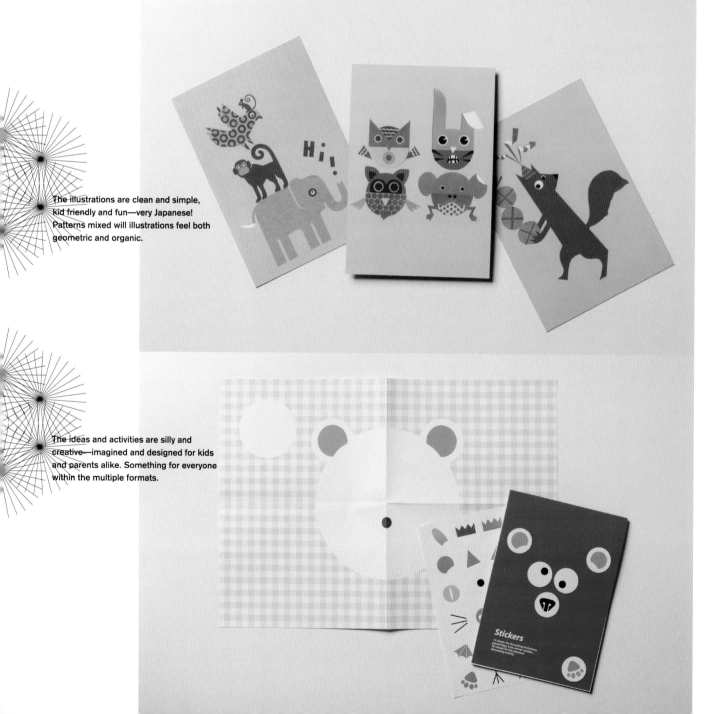

The ideas and activities are silly and
creative—imagined and designed for kids
and parents alike. Something for everyone
within the multiple formats.

104

Designer's Statement:

BRIEF

We were asked to create a children's party pack for the British Heart Foundation.

OBJECTIVES

The aim was to offer a party pack featuring games and recipes with a healthy twist. The packs include themed recipe cards, ideas for games and craft activities, and advice on preparing for a party. The challenge was to make the pack appeal to kids purely as a piece of fun, while communicating the underlying health messages effectively to parents.

DESIGN STRATEGY

We employed Lizzie Harris, professional chef turned writer and food stylist, to come up with party food ideas with an animal-themed twist, including carrot cakes that look like rabbits, sandwiches styled as chickens and buffalos, and a lion made out of tortilla chips. Photographer John Ross shot them all on paper plates, complete with crumbs and splats, to make everything look achievable and homemade.

The animal theme carried through into the party games turning traditional favorites like Egg and Spoon into Dinosaur Egg And Spoon, and Balloon Stomp into Pop Goes the Weasel. These were all illustrated by Rebecca Sutherland, using cut paper to continue the arts and crafts feel, while playful game instructions by Nick Asbury added to the sense of fun. We also designed items for the party itself, including invitations, placemats, and stickers, which can be used to decorate everything from goody bags to pieces of fruit. Debbie Allen, who leads the BHF's work with children and young people, said, "The playful and colorful design allows us to get over our serious messages about healthy eating in a deliciously fun and interactive way."

Title: Getxophoto 2011
Firm: IS Creative Studio
Art Director: Richars Meza
Designers: Richars Meza, Serena Gravili,
Lucia Merlo
Client: Getxophoto
Client Industry: Arts/Culture

Printer: Artes Gráficas Palermo
Method: Offset Stochastic
Paper: Coral Plus 112 gr
Color: 4 color + varnish

Fonts: Paper chain type, Helvetica Neue

Designer's Statement:

Getxophoto is a festival dedicated to photography that takes place in Getxo (Basque
Country) and supports the exploration of
formats, stands, and unconventional exhibition
spaces to show the different images.

The 2011 festival curated by Frank Kalero, has
the theme "In Praise of Elderly."

For the design we thought that the cross-stitch
was a great idea to represent the elderly. We
came up with a version of "Helvetica Stitched."
The poster was designed in Photoshop and
then given to a professional in the cross-stitch
media in Madrid to knit it on paper. The client
loved the design and the cross stitching in a
contemporary style.

For the communication pieces, the designers
made a cross-stitch typography as well for all
the signage. They stitched the Helvetica typeface and photographed it for all signage and
exhibition graphics. The result was a handmade
bold and yet warm identity.

Title: Getxophoto 2010
Firm: IS Creative Studio
Art Director: Richars Meza
Designers: Richars Meza, Angélica Montes, Luna Kadima
Client: Getxophoto
Client Industry: Cultural

Printer: Artes Gráficas Palermo
Method: Offset Stochastic
Paper: Coral Plus 112gr
Color: 4 color + varnish

Fonts: Paper chain type, Helvetica Neu

Designer's Statement:

The 2010 Getxophoto festival curated by Frank Kalero, with the theme "In praise of leisure," and it is about this moment dedicated to self-realization.

The signage it is based on the typography Paper Chain Type, created by the designers. As in the poster with the logo done in cut paper, folded and photographed, Paper Chain Type the designers created as strings of paper dolls we did as a child.

Title: Gráfika
Firm: IS Creative Studio
Art Director: Richars Meza
Designers: Richars Meza, Alice Spadaro
Client: Instituto Cervantes Madrid
Client Industry: Arts/Culture

Printer: Artes Gráficas Palermo
Method: Offset Stochastic
Paper: Coral Plus 125 gr
Color: 4 color

Font: Incognito Typeface

Designer's Statement:

Gráfika is an exhibition organized by the Instituto Cervantes, an institution that was founded by the Spanish government in 1991 to promote the Spanish language and Spanish and Hispanic-American culture. The central head office of the institution is located in Madrid, with more than fifty centers all over the world.

The brief was to create a graphic image for the exhibition Gráfika that moves in the context of Spanish urban culture. The city is their inspiration and workshop. The exhibition translates what is happening on walls and streets of our cities to an exhibition hall and explores the global movement called "street art."

Thirty Spanish artists will be showing their work on an exhibition of paintings, gratify, art performances, videos, objects, installations and sculptures.

The challenge is to create a bold, clear logo, avoiding clichés and creating an image that stands out from the artists' work.

The logotype and "Incognito Typography" was developed, inspired by the videos documenting street art. The street artists' faces are pixilated to protect their anonymity; we have pixellated the top of the typography; also, we have used the colors of the night-vision camcorders.

For the communication pieces, we played with big and small typography to give rhythm and funky style.

Title: Théâtre de la Minoterie (Marseilles)
Firm: Johann Hierholzer
Client: Théâtre de la Minoterie (Marseilles)

Method: Offset
Paper: Condat Matt Perigord PEFC (115 g)

Photographer: Philippe Houssin

Designer's Statement:

La Minoterie, Theater of la Joliette, opened in 1985. Because of the political and economic issues in the city of Marseilles, it will be destroyed very soon. Thanks to the tenacity of the theatrical company, it will be rebuilt a little further on the Port of la Joliette. These three programs 2011–2012 should show to the public that the old building still existed for this season (*C'est là* "Here"), and that it would be completely rebuilt soon (*Bientôt là* "Soon there") in the vast building site of Euroméditerranée between giant and up-to-date offices and car parks. The photo montage between the place and a ferry describes the link of the Theater with the Port of la Joliette but also describes of a beginning of destruction and reconstruction. All this is reinforced with humor by giant letters that recall the grandiose and megalomaniac sceneries of Hollywood studios.

Simple typography that varies from one column to two columns alludes to a complex yet flexible grid, adding to the rhythms established by the artwork.

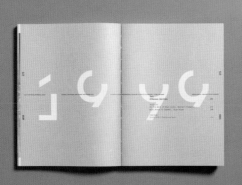

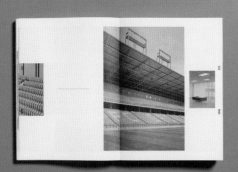

Title: Wiel Arets Architects, Stills
Firm: Mainstudio
Art Director: Edwin van Gelder
Client: Wiel Arets Architects
Client Industry: Architecture

Printer: Robstolk

Photographer: Jan Bitter

Designer's Statement:

The book *Stills—Wiel Arets, a Timeline of Ideas, Articles & Interviews 1982–2010* is about Dutch architect Wiel Arets. Typography plays a major role. It dictates the structure of the book with single-column pages in Aperçu bold for the texts written by Arets, and two-column pages in Aperçu Mono for articles by others. Also, typography reflects the chronology of the content. The dates that form the chapters of the book become more complete as the book progresses. Texts and images are on a chronological grid, and unfold along a horizontal timeline. The idea of a timeline is also suggested by the texts that begin in the middle of the page.

Intriguing photography speaks to vastness and geometry. The black-and-white images change in scale, cross folds, and bleed off edges.

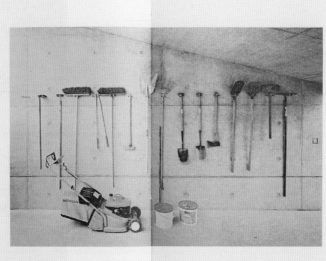

Title: White Lofts
Firm: Marius Fahrner Design
Art Director: Marius Fahrner
Designers: Marius Fahrner, Falco Hannemann
Client: GFG – Günther Franke Gruber,
Developers (Christoph Gruber)
Client Industry: Real estate

Method: Offset
Color: 4 color + 2 color, Hotfoil Silver

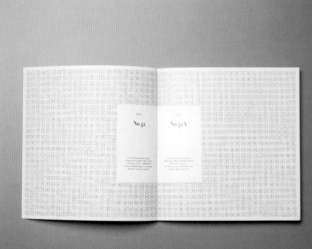

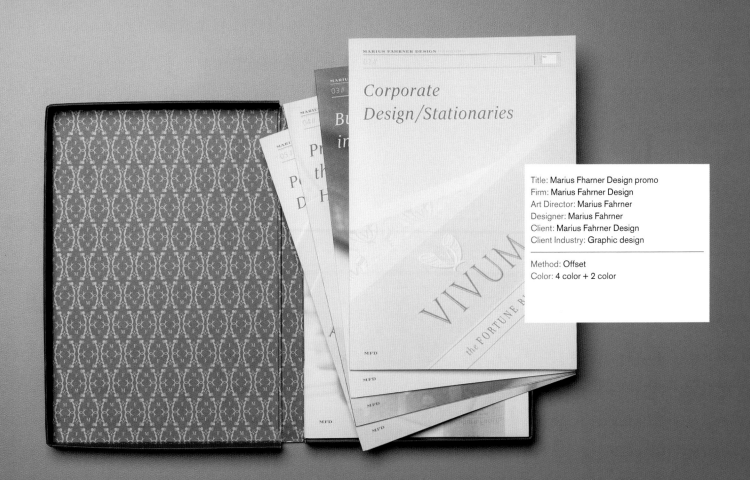

Title: Marius Fharner Design promo
Firm: Marius Fahrner Design
Art Director: Marius Fahrner
Designer: Marius Fahrner
Client: Marius Fahrner Design
Client Industry: Graphic design

Method: Offset
Color: 4 color + 2 color

Title: The Cries of San Francisco
Firm: MacFadden & Thorpe
Art Directors: Brett MacFadden, Scott Thorpe
Designer: Scott Thorpe
Client: Southern Exposure
Client Industry: Arts/Culture

Printer: Oscar Printing
Method: Offset
Paper: Gray 80 lb stock
Color: 2 color

Designer's Statement:

Folded poster/announcement for an exhibit and public work by the artist Allison Smith. Referencing street hawkers of earlier eras, Smith had a call for entry and chose sixty participants who each created a persona for the show. Several market days were held in the gallery, where they sold or gave away wares that could vary from eccentric art objects to services such as self-esteem boosting, culminating with a day-long event on San Francisco's main thoroughfare, Market Street. Our design gave participants their own seal on the poster, and these seals were also made into laser-cut wooden badges for each person to wear while performing.

FRANCISCO

2, 2011

MARKET DAY, PUBLIC ART EVENT
SATURDAY, JUNE 4, 12-5PM
Location: Mint Plaza & Market Street
between 3rd & 5th Streets

SOUTHERN EXPOSURE
HTTP://SOEX.ORG/CRIESOFSF
3030 20TH STREET
SAN FRANCISCO, CA
94110

PLEASE JOIN SOUTHERN EXPOSURE
FOR A PRIVATE MEMBERS' OPENING PREVIEW FOR
THE CRIES OF SAN FRANCISCO

A NEW EXHIBITION AND PUBLIC ART PROJECT BY ALLISON SMITH IN COLLABORATION WITH SOUTHERN EXPOSURE

FRIDAY, MAY 20, 2011
6:00-7:30PM
A public opening reception from 7:30 to 10:00PM will follow.
Beer generously provided by New Belgium.

Location:
SOUTHERN EXPOSURE
3030 20TH STREET, SAN FRANCISCO, CA 94110

RSVP
BY TUESDAY, MAY 17
to assocdirector@soex.org
or 415.863.2141

Members will have the first opportunity to pre-order
a limited edition print made by Allison Smith
for THE CRIES OF SAN FRANCISCO. Special thanks
to Paulson Bott Press and Haines Gallery.

TO MARKET TO MARKET!
ALLISON SMITH & SOUTHERN EXPOSURE
PRESENT

THE CRIES OF SAN FRANCISCO

MAY 20–JULY 2, 2011

THE CRIES OF SAN FRANCISCO

TIMELINE & PROJECT DETAILS

SATURDAY, JUNE 4, 2011
Market Day Public Art Event
12-5PM

Title: **Art Publishing Now**
Firm: **MacFadden & Thorpe**
Art Directors: **Brett MacFadden, Scott Thorpe**
Designer: **Brett MacFadden**
Client: **Southern Exposure**
Client Industry: **Arts/Culture**

Printer: **Oscar Printing**
Method: **Offset**
Paper: **white 80 lb stock**
Color: **2 color**

Designer's Statement:

Folded poster/announcement for a symposium and art fair focused on publishing for arts groups. The client wanted a modern take on a WPA poster, so a patriotic color scheme was used, with a stripe design that referenced the spine and cover of a book. In the mailed folded-down form, the piece looks like a little paperback.

Title: Alessandro Baldinotti
Firm: Studio Laura Moretti
Art Director: Laura Moretti
Designer: Laura Moretti
Client: Alessandro Baldinotti, actor

Paper: Coated matte
Color: Quadrichromie (4 colors)

Photographer: Private photo archive
Illustrator: Silvia Fabbroni
Writer: Alessandro Baldinotti

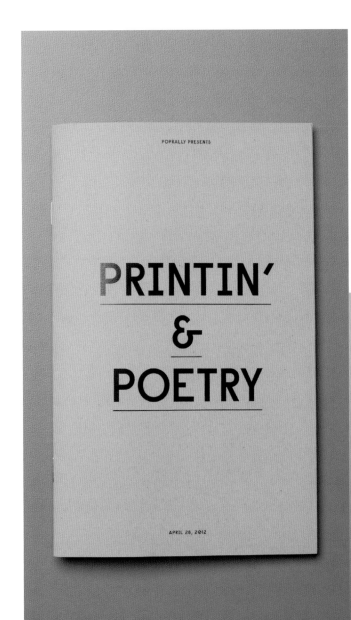

Title: Printin' & Poetry
Firm: Department of Advertising and
Graphic Design, The Museum of Modern Art
Creative Director: Julia Hoffmann
Art Director: Sam Sherman
Designer: Francesca Campanella
Production Manager: Althea Penza
Client: The Museum of Modern Art
Client Industry: Arts/Culture

Printer: The Copy Room
Method: 4 color Digital
Paper: Kraft smooth, light brown 65# cover and
Hammermill Smooth, White 50# text
Colors: 4/1, 4 color over black

Copy Editor: Carloyn Kelly

Title: Estoril Fashion Art Festival Catalogue
Firm: MusaWorkLab
Art Director: MusaWorkLab
Designer: MusaWorkLab
Client: Associação ModaLisboa
Client Industry: Fashion

Printer: M2 Artes Gráficas
Method: Offset
Paper: Fedrigoni paper

Fonts: Didot, League Gothic, Linux Libertine.
Photographers: Jornal O Século, C.M.Cascais,
Luciana Cristhovan, Eugenio Recuenco,
Jose Manuel Ferrater, David Urbano, Daniel
RierA, Antoine Passerat, Luis Venegas, Carlos
Ramos, Paulo Segadães, Luís de Barros, Pedro
Ferreira, Rui Aguiar
Illustrators: Maria Archer, MusaWorklab
Writers: Text by the authors

Designer's Statement:

Catalog for cultural festival that put together
Portuguese and Spanish creative talents such
as Luis Venegas, Paco Rabane

The festival incorporated exhibitions, fashion
shows and debates with names carefully sum-
moned from the ranks of fashion, photography,
publishing, cinema, video art, public art, and
food design.

The enclosing case is simple and
sophisticated with type debossed
giving it a high-end feel.

JOSÉ MANUEL FERRATER

EUGENIO RECUENCO

RIERA

CONVITE

TORIL

TOART

IVAL

LUIS

EXPOSIÇÃO

The variation in the cards reflects the
array of participants of the event.

Title: Estoril Fashion Art Festival Catalogue
Firm: MusaWorkLab

Although every card is quite different, the primary typeface and black/red/white color palette holds the pieces together visually.

JOSÉ MANUEL FERRATER
EUGENIO RECUENCO
DANIEL RIERA
DAVID URBANO

ETERNA
É A NOITE

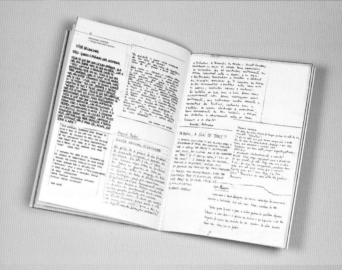

Title: Indústria series
Firm: MusaWorkLab
Art Director: MusaWorkLab
Designer: MusaWorkLab
Client: Indústria Club
Client Industry: Social

Printer: M2 Artes Gráficas
Method: Offset
Paper: Munken Lynx paper
Color: 2 color (spot)

Fonts: Tramp Gothic, Akkurat Mono, Umbro,
Lettera, Brauer Neue
Writers: Text by the authors

Designer's Statement:

Flyer and monthly club program for leading
Oporto nightclub

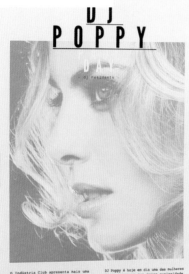

DJ
POPPY

DAS

dj residente

Sábado
23/Outubro

O Indústria Club apresenta mais uma
DJ no disparo de emoções da pista.
DJ Poppy é a convidada de Outubro.
Uma DJ que há já alguns anos percorre
algumas das cabinas nacionais, tendo
mesmo sido a DJ Revelação dos Night
Awards em 2003.
Para a DJ Poppy tudo começou no W,
club onde julgava que não seria apenas
mais do que sócia-gerente. Mas daí ao
salto para a cabina, onde o seu irmão
DJ Geninho era residente, foi a sua
própria grande surpresa.

DJ Poppy é hoje em dia uma das mulheres
DJ portuguesas que maior curiosidade
suscita ao crowd que a encara da pista,
nunca deixando de nos surpreender com
os seus House sets, e nunca nos deixando
esquecer que foi eleita em 2006 pela
Maxmen a DJ Mais Sexy portuguesa.
"The real girlie house style nite",
portanto, para ir ouvir com atenção
este sábado.

www.djpoppy.com
www.myspace.com/poppydj

Completamente rendido às sonoridades
mais electrónicas desde a sua
adolescência, DJ Vibe é o artista que
em 2010 nos faz continuar a acreditar
na música, nos ambientes de festa,
no foco essencial da Club Culture.

O DJ e produtor português a quem todos
os méritos — nacionais e internacionais
— já foram amplamente reconhecidos
e premiados, DJ Vibe conta mais de 25
anos de batalhas ganhas, proporcionando-
nos agora — e pela primeira vez —
uma residência na cidade do Porto.

ALL
NIGHT
LONG

DJ VIBE

Sexta
29/Outubro

Naturalmente que as expectativas estão
assim todas em aberto, guiadas pela
mente de um DJ versátil, conhecedor,
teimoso, bem humorado e para quem —
acima de tudo — é na música que encontra
a sua essência de vida. House, Tech
House, mais funky, ou nem sempre tão
funky... poderão ser algumas das
pontuações por que se medem as 8 horas
de set a que DJ Vibe já nos habituou,
e que vão com certeza preencher a sua
noite no Indústria do Porto.

É pois chegado o tempo certo de celebrar
esta Club Culture com DJ Vibe, com
a certeza de uma entrega apaixonada
e a partilha de toda uma vida dedicada
à música e de culto assumidamente
adquirido.

www.djvibe.net
www.myspace.com/djvibept

Title: FUNZINE
Firm: MusaWorkLab
Art Director: MusaWorkLab
Designer: MusaWorkLab
Client: MusaWorkLab
Client Industry: Graphic Design/promo

Printer: In house production
Method: photocopy
Paper: Fluo colored paper
Colors: Black + red photocopy spot color

Fonts: Musa-600, Times
Photographer: MusaWorkLab
Illustrator: MusaWorkLab
Writer: Wikipedia

Designer's Statement:

Graphic fanzine for MusaWorkLab
self-promotion

Title: Home & Abroad Catalog
Firm: MusaWorkLab
Art Director: MusaWorkLab
Designer: MusaWorkLab
Client: Xerem/Triangle Network
Client Industry: Arts/Culture

Printer: Gráfica Maiadouro
Methods: Offset (text), silkscreen (cover)
Paper: Hard cover on 2 mm gray card stock

Fonts: Akzidenz Grotesk, Neuzeit,
Process Grotesque
Photography: by the 25 artists
Writers: Alessio Antoniolli, Andrzej Raszyk,
David-Alexandre Guéniot, Fabrice Ziegler,
Herwig Turk, João Dias, Jorge Barreto Xavier,
Jorge Rocha, José António Fernandes Dias,
Lourenço egreja, Lúcia MArques, Mónica de
Miranda

Designer's Statement:

Art catalog for an international artists workshop

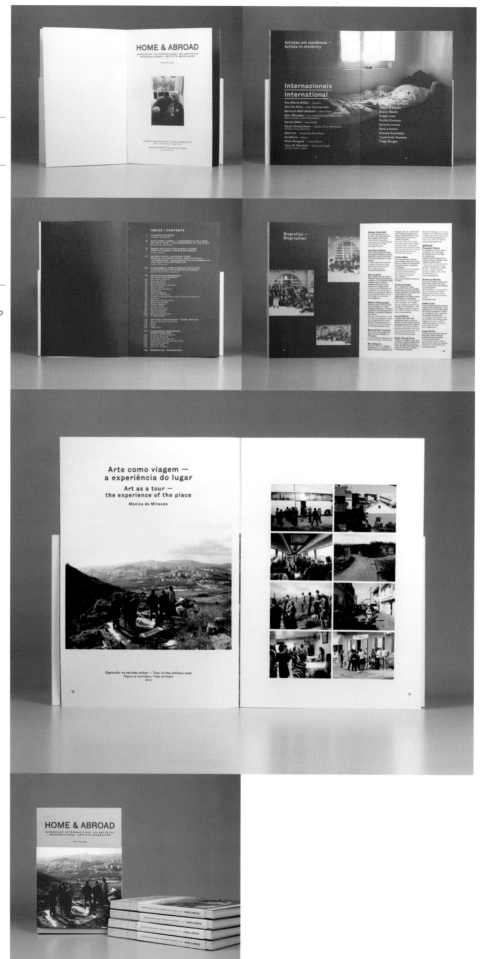

124

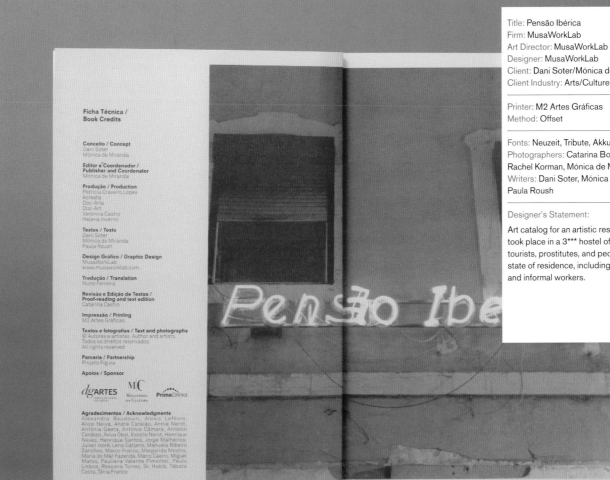

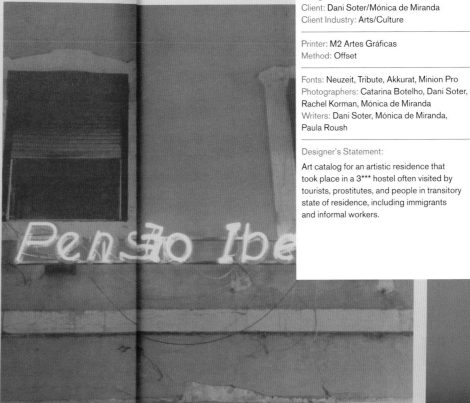

Ficha Técnica /
Book Credits

Conceito / Concept
Dani Soter
Mónica de Miranda

**Editor e Coordenador /
Publisher and Coordenator**
Mónica de Miranda

Produção / Production
Patricia Craveiro Lopes
Acresta
Doc-Arte
Doc-Art
Verónica Castro
Helena Inverno

Textos / Texts
Dani Soter
Mónica de Miranda
Paula Roush

Design Gráfico / Graphic Design
MusaWorkLab
www.musaworklab.com

Tradução / Translation
Nuno Ferreira

**Revisão e Edição de Textos /
Proof-reading and text edition**
Catarina Castro

Impressão / Printing
M2 Artes Gráficas

Textos e fotografias / Text and photographs
© Autores e artistas. Author and artists.
Todos os direitos reservados
All rights reserved

Parceria / Partnership
Projeto Figura

Apoios / Sponsor

dgARTES   MC Ministério da Cultura   PrimeDrinks

Agradecimentos / Acknowledgments
Alexandra Baudouin, Alexis Lefevre,
Alice Neiva, André Catalão, Annie Nerot,
Antónia Gaeta, António Câmara, António
Cardoso, Aviva Obst, Estelle Nerot, Henrique
Neves, Henrique Santos, Jorge Malheiros,
Julien Isoré, Lena Gätjens, Manuela Ribeiro
Sanches, Marco Franco, Margarida Mestre,
Maria do Mar Fazenda, Mário Caeiro, Miguel
Matos, Paubiana Valente Pimentel, Paulo
Lisboa, Rossana Torres, Sr. Habib, Tábata
Costa, Tânia Franco

Title: Pensão Ibérica
Firm: MusaWorkLab
Art Director: MusaWorkLab
Designer: MusaWorkLab
Client: Dani Soter/Mónica de Miranda
Client Industry: Arts/Culture

Printer: M2 Artes Gráficas
Method: Offset

Fonts: Neuzeit, Tribute, Akkurat, Minion Pro
Photographers: Catarina Botelho, Dani Soter,
Rachel Korman, Mónica de Miranda
Writers: Dani Soter, Mónica de Miranda,
Paula Roush

Designer's Statement:

Art catalog for an artistic residence that
took place in a 3*** hostel often visited by
tourists, prostitutes, and people in transitory
state of residence, including immigrants
and informal workers.

Paula Roush

Estéticas migratórias / conceitos viajantes /
epistemologia do lugar nómada

Migratory aesthetics / travelling concepts /
epistemology of the nomadic place

— II —

Title: SFBALLET—the 80th Season
Firm: Noon
Art Director: Cinthia Wen
Designer: Cinthia Wen
Client: San Francisco Ballet
Client Industry: Performing Arts

Title: Variance
Firm: Paperwhite Studio
Art Director: Isaac Gertman
Client: Variance
Client Industry: Fashion

Printer: Linco Printing
Method: Offset lithography
Colors: 2 color (black and red) + 4-color
process (insert)

Writers: Alfredo Brillembour,
Denise Hoffman Brandt (editors)

Designer's Statement:

Variance is a line of luxury jewelry that has a
secondary function: It can be used to express
evolving relationship dynamics. The lookbook
functions like the jewelry: Hidden between
product spreads are photographs that illustrate
an object's secondary use.

Title: Op ontdekking in een duurzame wereld/Werken in Eneco World
Firm: Ping-Pong Design
Art Director: Meike Nip
Designers: Eline Wieriks, Meike Nip
Client: Eneco energy
Client Industry: Energy

Printer: Opmeer drukkerij bv, Den Haag
Method: Offset
Paper: 130 gr Munken Lynx, 170 gr silk MC Cocoon, 90 gr recycled Cyclus offset, 283 gr adhesive paper
Color: 4 color

Font: Etelka
Photographers: Milan Vermeulen, Mieke Meesen, Annet Delfgaauw, Hans de Meij
Writers: Nelly Dijkstra, Anouk van Hemert

Designer's Statement:

The book functions as a travel guide for a new working environment. A 'Lonely Planet' for a smarter way of working.

128

Title: Are We There Yet?
Firm: Plazma Design
Art Director: Todd Hansson
Designer: Todd Hansson
Client: Wayfinding Australia
Client Industry: Construction

Printer: Cornerstone Press
Methods: Offset printing, foiling, diecutting
Paper: Doggetts Brilliant Smooth White
Colors: 4 color (soy-based inks) + 1 Pantone +
Satin Seal varnish + Laser foil

Fonts: Helvetica Neue, Close-CallPM
Photographer: Todd Hansson
Writer: Bryce Tolliday

Any successful wayfinding experience will involve a level of planning and assessment of one's abilities and available resources in relation to the journey to be undertaken.

Image is the connector that all good wayfinding designs are based upon. Image can be naturally occurring, it can be built and it can be applied. Designs which rely upon image will include elements which use human senses to allow cognitive recognition of location, space and destination.

Title: Tipping Point Annual Report
Firm: Public
Art Director: Todd Foreman
Designers: Todd Foreman, Lindsay Wheeler
Client: Tipping Point Community
Client Industry: Nonprofit

Printer: p.s. PrintSmart
Method: Offset
Paper: Mohawk Superfine
Color: 4 color

Font: Archer

Designer's Statement:

Tipping Point is a nonprofit dealing with poverty issues in the San Francisco Bay Area. This annual report uses a mix of colorful info graphics and personal stories to communicate the scale of the situation and how poverty affects people individually.

Title: Jonathan Sprague Photography Promo
Firm: Public
Art Director: Todd Foreman
Designer: Tessa Lee
Client: Jonathan Sprague Photography
Client Industry: Photography/promo

Printer: p.s. PrintSmart
Method: Offset
Color: 4 color

Fonts: American Typewriter
Photographer: Jonathan Sprague

Title: Products Re-imagined
Firm: R3 Lab/R3lab.org
Art Director: Tom Sieu
Designers: Andrew Johnson, Cristian
Butcovich, Judy Hsu, Emily Lemmer,
Jeanette Karthaus, Tomo Kaji
Client: Academy of Art University, R3 Lab
Client Industry: Academia, Design education

Printer: California Lithographer
Method: Traditional offset lithography
Paper: Mohawk Superfine
Colors: 4-color process + 2 pms

Writers: Each book is authored by respective
designer. Each designer was responsible for
written content as well as associated photography and/or illustration.

Designer's Statement:

R3 Lab is a collaborative effort by the
Academy of Art University's graphic design
students and faculty to promote social and
sustainable design. Each project included in
this ambitious collaboration examines product
life cycles and seeks to create more thoughtful,
long-term holistic solutions. The resulting collection of books showcases each designer's
innovative solutions—and how they directly
benefit people's lives. This forward-looking
project demonstrates design's integral part in
changing patterns.

This is a nice collection of booklets with
an eclectic approach to the typography,
photography, and illustration. Obviously a lot
of fun for the students and faculty to work
together on.

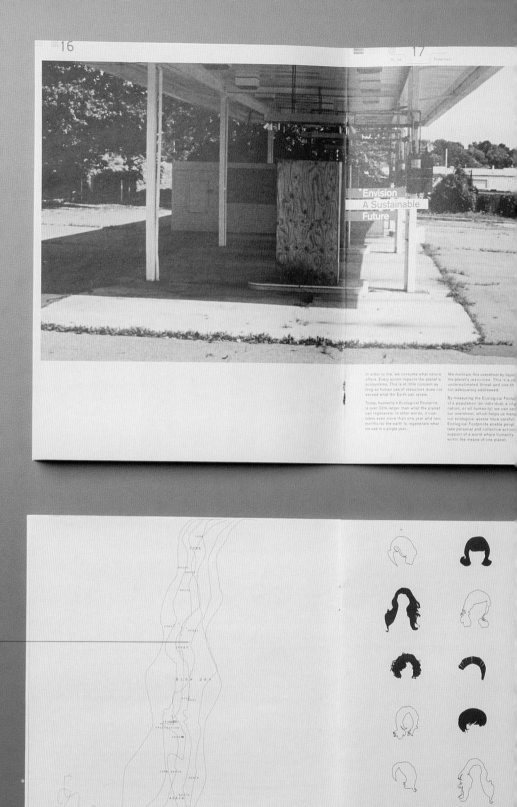

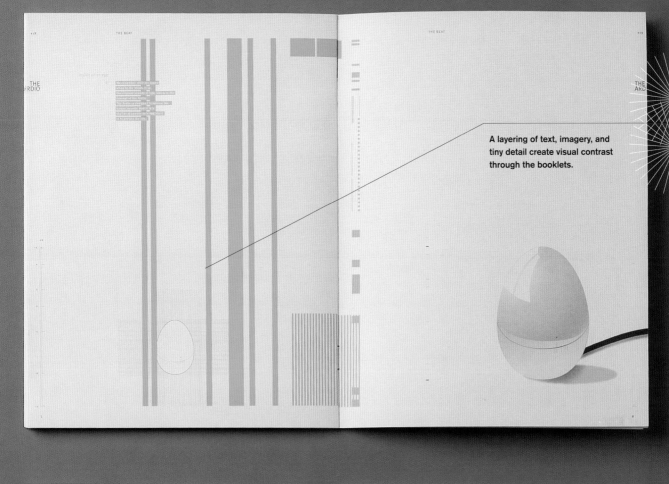

A layering of text, imagery, and tiny detail create visual contrast through the booklets.

Beautiful integration of type and image.

Title: The Cove
Firm: Rubber Design
Designer: Jacquie Van Keuren
Client: Hutner Group, Emerald Fund
Client Industry: Real Estate

Printer: Hemlock Printers
Methods: Offset printing, Custom Duplex Paper
with tip on
Paper: Neenah Classic Crest, Custom duplex
with String & Button
Colors: 5 color over 5 color

Fonts: Formata, Minion Pro

Designer's Statement:

This brochure kit was designed for Hutner
Group, leveraging The Cove branding they
established. The piece offers a very flexible
system for customizing kits to individual buyers'
tastes in floor plans and property location.

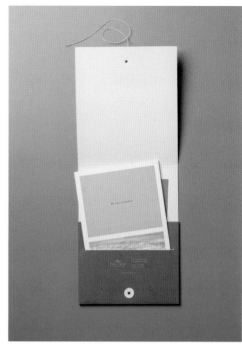

TURNS OUT

YOU CAN TEACH AN OLD...

OTHER OB...

ASTROMETRY, PHO...

CYCLICAL

TIMELESS
DEPENDAB
TECHNOLOGY

YOU CAN ACHIEVE

STELLAR RESULTS WITH VINTAGE TOOLS

Title: Dependable Letterpress Promotion
Firm: Rubber Design
Designer: Jacquie Van Keuren
Client: Dependable Letterpress
Client Industry: Printing/promo

Printer: Dependable Letterpress
Method: Letterpress
Paper: Mohawk Renewal and Synergy
(Now–Loop)
Colors: 5 color over 2 color

Fonts: Eyechart, Radio, Gotham, Numbers:
Greenback, P22 Petemoss, Letterhead Fonts:
Dickinson, Boston Truckstyle, Full Bloc, Fire
House, Tonic Nerve
Writer: Carol Miller, Rubber Design

Designer's Statement:
The concept for this piece comes from Joel
Benson of Dependable Letterpress—both the
visual inspiration of vintage planetary charts
and the device, a perpetual calendar. He
wanted to play with color well outside of the
more budget-conscious one or two-color work
he finds himself doing more often than not.

Title: Go/Give
Firm: Studio 2br
Art Director: David Shalam
Designer: Daniel Hayes
Client: Deutsche Bank
Client Industry: Financial Services

Printer: Westerham Press
Methods: Litho, Screen print
Paper: Fenner Paper Flint Colourset 270 gsm
(cover), Fenner Paper Offenbach Bible 40 gsm
(text)
Colors: 4-color process + 1 PMS

Fonts: Univers, Deutsche Bank
Photographers: Nick David, John Wildgoose,
Lee Mawdsley
Writer: Stuart Daniel

Give

Give yourself a new experience
If more people volunteer we can do more to he
and take on even bigger challenges. Do you?
Why not get the rest of the team involved?

Give to good causes
Our Charities of the Year, The Eve Appeal and
War Child, need ambassadors, fundraisers,
promoters and donors. Which could you be?
Can we beat the £1.76m raised in 2010?

Give up your salary
Only 10% of employees give tax efficiently
through payroll giving. Why not improve the
effectiveness of your charitable donations?

Give us a ring
We'd love to chat about how we can get you
engaged in what we do and make your time
at Deutsche Bank more fulfilling.
Call 020 7545 7904.

Interesting format in that the book flips
halfway through between "Give" and "Go."
Feels like two books in one. The paper adds
to the intrigue—almost as thin as tissue.

Simple text is a nice complement to the pattern and beautiful photography.

Title: Neue Galerie Catalog
Firm: Tenazas Design
Art Director: Lucille Tenazas
Designer: Lucille Tenazas
Client: Neue Galerie, Museum for German and
Austrian Art, New York
Client Industry: Museum

Fonts: Neue Bold, Berthold Akzidenz Grotesk
Photographers: Hulya Kolabas, Annie
Schlecter, Neue Galerie

Concept: Renée Price
Production Manager: Anna Truxes
Editorial: Scott Gutterman, Janis Staggs,
Christian Witt-Dörring
Stylist: Paul Landy
Assistant Stylist: Colleen Kinneary

Printer: DigiLink, Alexandria, VA
Method: Offset

Designer's Statement:

The square format follows an existing system
that was developed for the Neue Galerie
Design Shop catalog starting in 2001 when the
museum opened. Our design improvement was
the creation of a grid system that established a
hierarchy between descriptive text and product
images. With this issue, we began the use
of pattern and period graphics for the cover,
stamped with the iconic Neue Galerie logo in
the center.

Our long-standing relationship with the
museum has afforded us an opportunity to
refine, rethink, and redesign succeeding brochures in ways that track our evolving design
process.

Concept: Renée Price
Creative Director: Paul Landy
Editorial: Scott Gutterman, Wilhelm Stabenau,
Janis Staggs
Design Assistant: Daniela Polidura
Production Assistant: Carole Jeung

Printer: Finlay Printing, Bloomfield, CT
Method: Offset

Designer's Statement:

At 136 pages and its biggest catalog to date,
the Design Shop celebrates the 10th anniversary of the Neue Galerie. New layout features
include a series of product still lifes with vellum
overlays that serve as a form of indexing and
product reference. The series continues with
the use of a Josef Hoffman–designed wallpaper
on the cover.

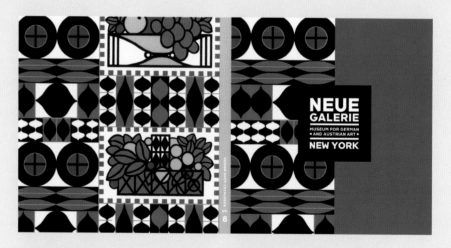

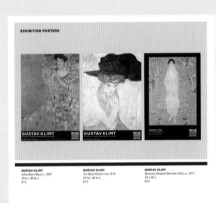

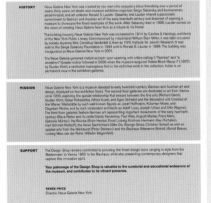

Title: **Parsons/The New School for Design**
Firm: **Tenazas Design**
Art Director: **Lucille Tenazas**
Designer: **Lucille Tenazas**
Design Assistant: **Candice Ralph**
Client: **Parsons The New School for Design
School of Constructed Environments, New York**
Client Industry: **Education/Academia**

Printer: **Donald Blyler Offset, Lebanon, PA**
Method: **Offset**

Fonts: **Din, Franklin Gothic demi**
Photographers: **Various**
Editorial: **Joanna Merwood-Salisbury**

Designer's Statement:

The poster within the brochure format creates a two-prong information system that each serves a unique purpose: The brochure details the individual programs within Parsons's School of Constructed Environments and the poster serves as the image piece that projects a cohesive design ethos under one collective umbrella.

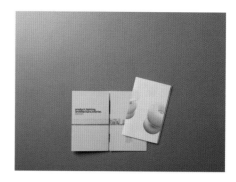

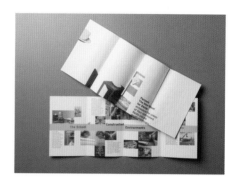

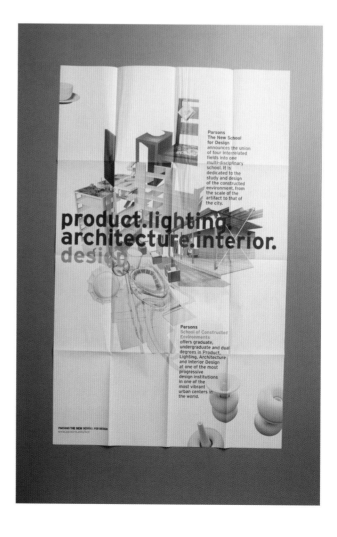

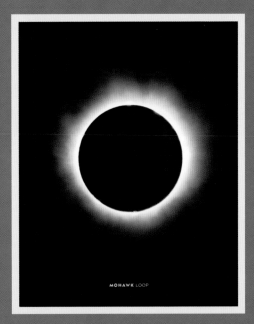

MOHAWK LOOP

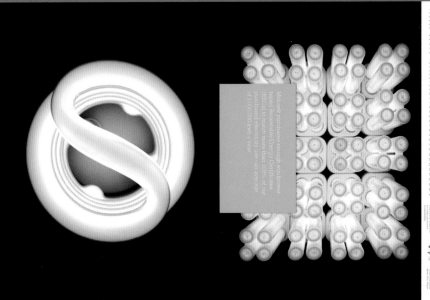

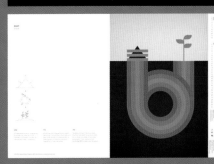

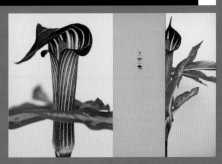

Title: Mohawk Loop
Firm: Tomorrow Partners
Art Director: Gaby Brink
Designers: Mónica Hernández, Scott Hickman, Amber Reed
Client: Mohawk Fine Papers

Printer: RR Donnelley, Wetmore Plant, Houston, TX
Paper: Mohawk Loop

Fonts: Akzidenz Grotesque, Gotham, Rockwell, Omnes
Photographers: Ron van Dongen, Steve Cohen, Misha Ashton, Laurie Frankel, Daniel Geiseke, Blaise Hayward, Kane Longden, Tier Und Naturfotografie J & C Sohns, Getty Images; Katherine Wolkoff, Art & Commerce; Michael Hall, Getty Images
Writers: Nathalie Destandau, Natalie Linden, Wendy Jedlicka, Jason McVay

Designer's Statement:

Mohawk's purchase of the SMART brands formed the most extensive collection of PCW papers on the market. Tomorrow's challenge: to name, position, and launch the amalgam line as the go-to collection of PCW papers, with an unquestionable environmental pedigree backed by Mohawk's decades-long commitment to sustainable business practices.

All the Mohawk Loop communication materials–Living Almanac promo, swatchbook, launch site, ad campaign–express a joyful, celebratory vibe. The imagery starts with the as-yet-unharnessed powers of nature (solar eclipse) and progresses to human conservation (CFL lightbulb, pinwheel made from newspaper): the full spectrum of sustainable opportunity. And the content and tone, as expressed in the tagline "Beautiful paper. Bright ideals." focuses not on guilt, responsibility, or those ubiquitous "eco tips," but on the positive outlook and impact of the line.

Tilte: your solutions Here
Firm: Volume Inc.
Art Directors: Adam Brodsley, Eric Heiman
Designer: Eric Heiman
Client: Mohawk Fine Papers
Client Industry: Paper

Printer: The Hennegan Company
Method: Offset, clear and metallic foil stamp
Papers: Mohawk Solutions, (various weights, colors and finishes)
Colors: 4 color + 3 PMS, metallic foil stamp (interior dividers), 2 PMS + foil stamp (cover)

Fonts: Tungsten, Courier Sans, Berthold Akzidenz Grotesk, Didot, Numbers Strasse & Dividend, Sentinel, Foundry Gridnik, Lettres Ornées
Photographers: Various (see colophon for full credits)
Writers: Robin Sloan, Brian McMullen, Jesse Nathan, Larry Smith, Carol Miller, Eric Heiman

Designer's Statement:

Mohawk's Solutions line is primarily pitched at in-house design teams creating corporate materials and projects on a budget. The promotion is a teaching guide to inspire designers to think expansively about how mundane source material can sing if looked at in new ways.

We randomly selected ten images and intuitively compiled them into an image sequence that would repeat three times. Next, we gave the sequence to three writers who each wrote his or her own narrative to accompany it.

We designed to each written piece while still maintaining the same image layout throughout all three sequences. It's the "Groundhog Day" paper promotion—it always starts in the same place, but the three outcomes are different, illustrating the disparate ways one could approach a design problem using the same source material.

We love the concept behind this piece. The way it starts from the same source and ends up with three totally different solutions.

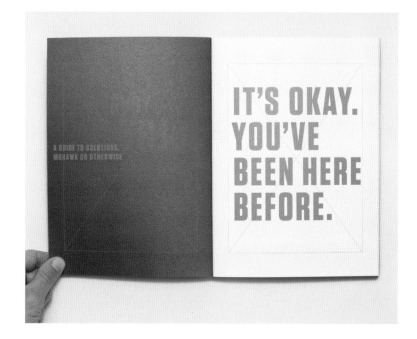

Pacing and rhythm insure each turn of the page makes you catch your breath.

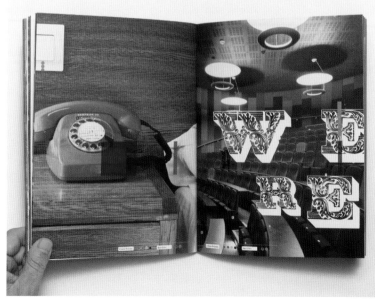

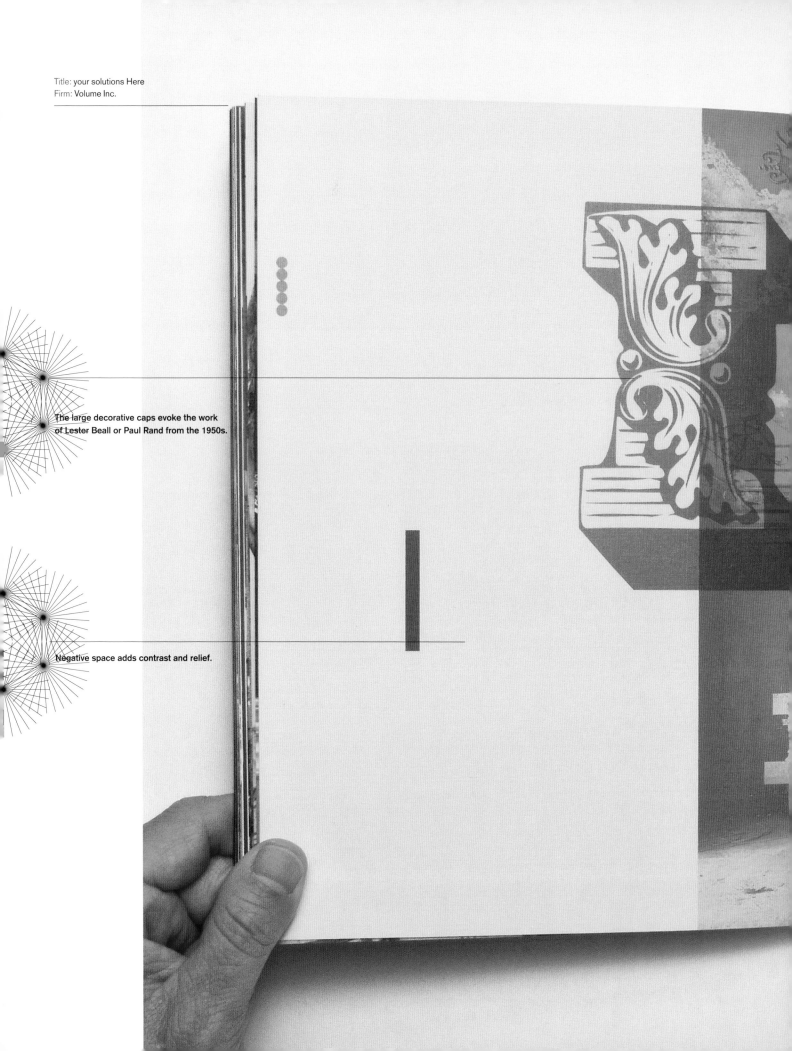

The large decorative caps evoke the work
of Lester Beall or Paul Rand from the 1950s.

Negative space adds contrast and relief.

We love all the layering of typogphy and color over the imagery. The metallic ink is opaque but some of the image still shows through, creating a layered richness.

Color Process

Spot Color

Title: Pivot/AIGA design conference
Firm: Volume Inc.
Art Directors: Adam Brodsley, Eric Heiman
Designer: Eric Heiman, Brice McGowen, Daniel Amara (Pivot typeface)
Client: AIGA
Client Industry: Graphic Design

Printer: O'Neil Printing
Method: Offset
Papers: Neenah Starwhite (cover), Environment (interior), Natural, Smooth
Color: 4 color

Fonts: Custom, Egyptienne, Gravur Condensed

Designer's Statement:

The "Pivot" theme of the 2011 AIGA National Conference focused on the rapidly evolving state of design. The identity, with its multiple logos and triple-weight typeface, provides a rich palette with which to design. Its energy and versatility also reflect the urgency for designers to be professionally nimble, and the multiple channels designers must all embrace in order to succeed.

The program "pivots" itself by having two covers and two opposite-orientated sections inside, separated by a set of stickers that attendees used to create messages in the program, on their badges, and who knows where else.

HET ACHTSTE WERELD-WONDER

MARC VAN DIJK

1648 – HEDEN

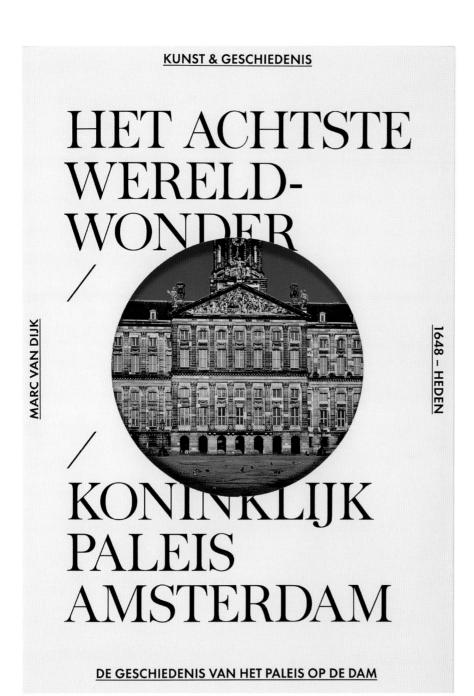

KONINKLIJK PALEIS AMSTERDAM

DE GESCHIEDENIS VAN HET PALEIS OP DE DAM

Title: Royal Palace Amsterdam
Firm: Vanessa van Dam
Designer: Vanessa van Dam
Client: Koninklijk Paleis Amsterdam (Royal Palace Amsterdam)
Client Industry: Arts/Culture

Printer: Tuijtel, Hardinxveld-Giessendam
Method: full-color
Paper: Arctic Volume White, special: cut-out circle on cover
Color: 4 color

Font: Futura

Designer's Statement:

The Royal Palace was originally built in 1648 as a town hall for Amsterdam. In 1808 Napoleon's brother, Louis Napoleon, had become the king of Holland and decided to make the Town Hall his residence. When the French Empire came to an end, it kept the function of a Palace. Nowadays it is one of the Palaces used by the Dutch Royal House, notably for State Visits and other official functions. When the Palace is not in use by the Royal House, it is open to the public. Twice a year an exhibition is on show.

I wanted to contextualize the history of the Royal Palace in a wider perspective. By reviewing the little black-and-white pictures in the margins of each text page, you get to know about what was happening in Amsterdam or even in the world in a specific period.

In this way you can read about tulips, wars, colonies, artists, city population, and so forth.

This information becomes a second layer of information, which helps you understand the history of the Palace.

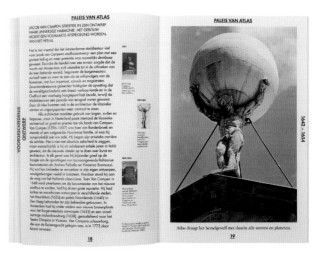

No two people are the same.

Calgary Society for Persons with Disabilities
2005 Annual Report

Some solutions are modest.

We encourage our clients to be active as much as is possible, and one particular bowler is so enthused he can't bring himself to let our staff win.

AND OTHERS ARE LOFTY.

NO TWO NEEDS ARE EXACTLY THE SAME.

That's why not all of our caregiving solutions are the same

THE BEACH BOYS

take one client to a staff volunteered of their own.

Some solutions a

Some are small

In some cases, finding that favourite Teddy bear can bring a world of warmth.

and others big

FOR ANOTHER CLIENT WE WERE ABLE TO GO ONE STEP FURTHER, AND FOUND A PLACE FOR HER SISTER, JUST NEXT DOOR.

and some are more complex.

NO TWO
ARE EX
THE SAM

SOME SOLUTIONS ARE SIMPLE.

Bringing music into the life of one of our clients has given them hours of happiness.

In order to take one music-loving client to a concert our staff volunteered countless hours of their own.

So

but all of our solutions are the same in one way — each and every one is personalized. because we know one size never fits all.

Title: Calgary Society for Persons with Disabilities 2011 Annual Report
Firm: WAX
Creative Director: Joe Hospodarec
Design Director: Monique Gamache
Designer: Hans Thiessen
Client: Calgary Society for Persons with Disabilities (CSPD)

Printer: Blanchette Press

Photographer: Brad Connell
Illustrators: Alexander Sakarev, Brad Connell, Dan Wright, Greg Thompson, Hans Thiessen, Joe Hospodarec, Max May, Monique Gamache, Shayne McBride, Theresa Kwan
Writers: Max May
Account Manager: Jackie Awada
Production Manager: Kelly Sembinelli

Designer's Statement:

The Calgary Society for Persons with Disabilities (CSPD) is a nonprofit organization, which provides residential care to adults with developmental disabilities. What truly separates the CSPD is its ability to provide each of its clients with custom, personalized care giving. To showcase this tailored approach, we created a report filled with pages of different shapes, sizes, and textures. To further demonstrate this, the report also incorporates the individual handwriting of nearly a dozen separate people.

Different papers and print styles add to the feel of a collection of found objects.

Title: Tomorrow—SAPPI Ideas that
Matter—2012 call for entries
Firm: Weymouth Design
Art Directors: Arvi Raquel-Santos,
Bob Kellerman
Designer: Arvi Raquel-Santos
Client: Sappi Fine Paper
Client Industry: Paper

Printer: Hemlock Printers
Method: Offset lithography
Papers: Sappi McCoy Silk 100 lb (cover),
100 lb (text)
Colors: 7/7, 4-color process + 2 PMS +
spot satin varnish

Font: Helvetica Neue
Photographer: Michael Weymouth
Writers: Delphine Hirasuna, Weymouth Design

Designer's Statement:

Ideas that Matter is the industry's only grant
program that recognizes and supports designers who generously donate their time and talent
to a wide range of charitable causes. Since
1999, Ideas that Matter has funded over 500
nonprofit projects, contributing $12 million
worldwide to causes that affect our lives and
our communities. The 2012 call for entries illustrates the story that Today/Tomorrow designers
are creating meaningful and impactful work.
More importantly, we wanted to focus on the
idea that all designers have an opportunity to
use their talent for the greater good.

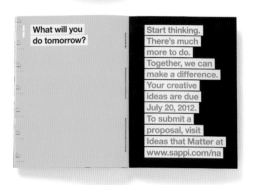

SLICK TYPOGRAPHY · PRETTY PICTURES

DESIGN IS NOT

DESIGN IS HOPE MADE VISIBLE

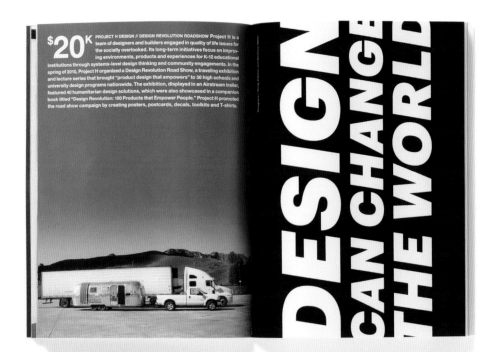

$20K PROJECT H DESIGN // DESIGN REVOLUTION ROADSHOW Project H is a team of designers and builders engaged in quality of life issues for the socially overlooked. Its long-term initiatives focus on improving environments, products and experiences for K-12 educational institutions through systems-level design thinking and community engagements. In the spring of 2010, Project H organized a Design Revolution Road Show, a traveling exhibition and lecture series that brought "product design that empowers" to 36 high schools and university design programs nationwide. The exhibition, displayed in an Airstream trailer, featured 40 humanitarian design solutions, which were also showcased in a companion book titled "Design Revolution: 100 Products that Empower People." Project H promoted the road show campaign by creating posters, postcards, decals, toolkits and T-shirts.

DESIGN CAN CHANGE THE WORLD

Title: Design is not—SAPPI Ideas that Matter—2011 call for entries
Firm: Weymouth Design
Art Directors: Arvi Raquel-Santos, Bob Kellerman
Designer: Arvi Raquel-Santos
Client: Sappi Fine Paper
Client Industry: Paper

Printer: Hemlock Printers
Method: Offset lithography
Papers: Sappi McCoy Silk 100 lb (cover), 100 lb (text)
Color: 7/7, 4-color process + 2 PMS + spot satin varnish

Fonts: Helvetica Neue
Photographer: Michael Weymouth, Rob Villanueva
Writers: Delphine Hirasuna, Weymouth Design

DESIGN PLAYS A ROLE IN TELLING THE HUMAN STORY

DESIGN HAS THE POWER TO CREATE MASSIVE CHANGE

Matt Rollins // Iconologic // Atlanta, GA

Doug Powell // Schwartz Powell // Minneapolis, MN

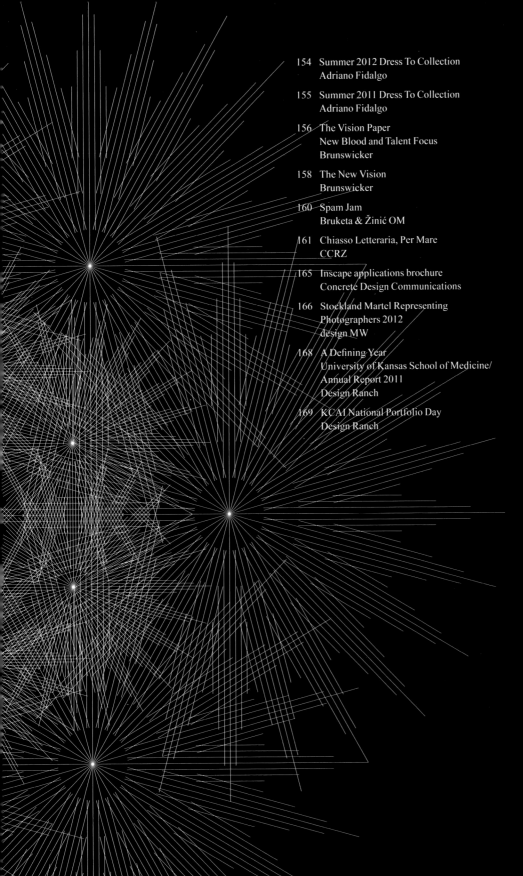

Title: Summer 2012 Dress To Collection
Firm: Adriano Fidalgo
Art Director: Adriano Fidalgo
Designer: Adriano Fidalgo
Client: Dress To
Client Industry: Fashion

Printer: Burti
Method: Offset
Papers: DuoDesign Suzano, Alta Alvura
Alcalino Suzano

Font: Helvetica Neue
Photographer: Luciano Quintella
Illustrator: Adriano Fidalgo

Statement:

The theme of summer 2012 collection was about the colorful Vietnam; thus, the childrens' catalog was designed in a pop-up format based on origami art. The colors are as vibrant as the country nature, fruits, and garments.

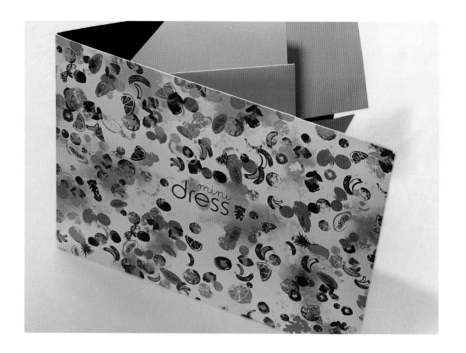

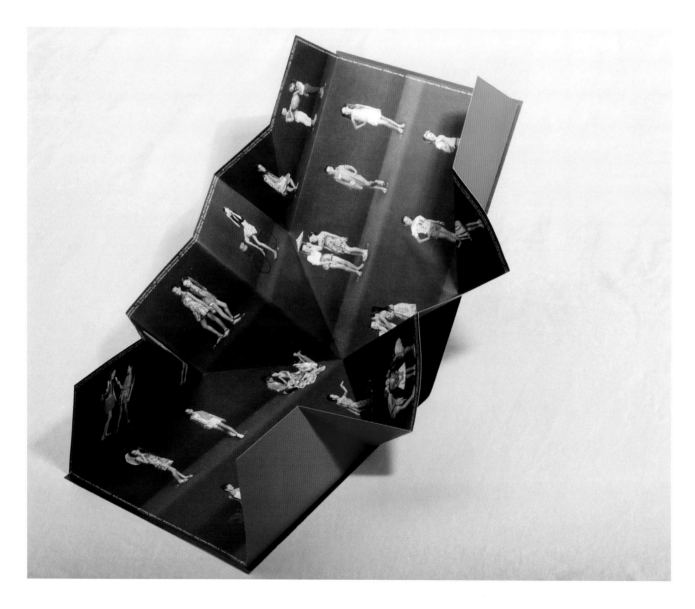

Title: Summer 2011 Dress To Collection
Firm: Adriano Fidalgo
Art Director: Adriano Fidalgo
Designer: Adriano Fidalgo
Client: Dress To
Client Industry: Fashion

Printer: Burti
Method: Offset
Papers: Alta Alvura Alcalino Suzano,
DuoDesign Suzano

Fonts: Caviar Dreams, Kus Script
Photographer: Eduardo Rezende
Illustrator: Adriano Fidalgo

Statement:

The theme of summer 2011 collection was
about good memories; thus, the catalog was
designed as a big vintage letter envelope with
twelve big postcards. The colors range from
pastels to faded shades.

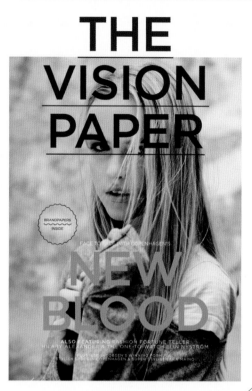

THE
VISION
PAPER

BRANDPAPERS
INSIDE

FACE TO FACE WITH COPENHAGEN'S

NEW
BLOOD

ALSO FEATURING FASHION FORTUNE TELLER
HILARY ALEXANDER & THE ONE-TO-WATCH ELIN NYSTRÖM
PLUS MDS JACOBSEN'S WINNING FORMULA
STYLISH MEN IN COPENHAGEN & SUPER STYLIST MARA MAINO

COPENHAGEN FASHION WEEK. AW2012

N

NATASHA SKOU

HOW DID YOU GET STARTED I
worked at Georg Jensen, which is
So I actually grew up with Danish
I was 18.
Later I become fashion buyer and
Cph Vision team. Working internat
I couldn't ask for more."

HOW WOULD YOU DESCRIBE I
Every new day brings fresh challe

WHAT DOES A NORMAL DAY L
WEEK? "It starts early. First, I see
Then it's off to the fair where I wa
We organise the seating for the gu
if H.R.H. Crown Princess Mary is
on security and press, and so that
international journalists and bloggs
and are connecting with their inne
There's also a lot of updating on s
releases to stay on top of during th
then it's home to give my boyfriend
starts over again."

WHAT ARE YOUR MOST IMPO
press database, the web in general
I am a very curious person, so gai
of inspiration that I can use in my

WHY DO YOU THINK COPENH
REGION'S LEADING FASHION E
and interesting on several levels. E

LET'S DANCE!
Join us on Friday 3 February for the CPH Vision Party, sponsored by PIPER Champagne, Heineken
and Egekilde from Lipti. Pick up your invitation at the Press Desk at the trade fairs. See you there!
WWW.CPHVISION.DK

14 / 28

Layering different views creates both
mystery and revelation—this is how design
can make good photography even better.

An underlined sans serif creates a strong
visual brand for the series.

THE
VISION
PAPER

A MINIMAL FASHION PAPER FROM CPH VISION AND TERMINAL 2

FASHION'S FIRST LADY *Behind the Scenes*
MARVELLOUS MARC *that hates* AND MORE

TALENT
FOCUS

+ BEAUTY PICKS AND COPENHAGEN CITY GUIDE

BRANDPAPERS
INSIDE

COPENHAGEN FASHION WEEK. SS2012

JUERGEN TELLER   MARC JACOBS

MARC JACOBS ADVERTISING - JUNE 2008

THE
HOUSE
THAT
MARC
BUILT

IN 1986 THE FA
AND UNSPECT
LABEL, PRODU
AND THE MAN

WWW.MARCJACOBS.COM

The name
internation
the forefro
mens-, wor
accessorie
as well as
Mare by M
ready-to-w
Copenhag
opened in
has becom
and bags, a
With the a
the team h
an integra
the city th

FIVE TO WATCH

WORDS RASMUS FOLEHAVE HANSEN

ULTRA-COOL GERMAN DESIGN, NORTHERN KNITWEAR, FLAMBOYANT ITALIANS AND DANISH START-UPS, HERE ARE THE DESIGNERS TO KEEP AN EYE OUT FOR THIS SEASON.

UNRAVEL 19022010

Flamboyant, colourful, and beautifully draped rich fabrics – Unravel is quintessentially Italian. Margherita Brazzale and Giuseppe Fanelli have joined forces to create showstopping pieces guaranteed to turn heads at parties.

WWW.UNRAVEL19022010.COM

UCON

Keeping your laptop safe is a top priority. Ucon and carpenter Rainer Spehl have joined case to help you do just that. Their beautifully crafted case in leather-bound wood is the ideal travel companion for your precious hardware.
Additionally, the Germany-based label is firmly on track for the new season with its sporty collection of street-inspired t-shirts, hoodies and jackets for both sexes.

WWW.UCON-ACROBATICS.COM

HUNKØN

Founded by Anne Skovgaard Schøler, Hunkøn is located in Hangzhou, China. An avid student of fabrics, Anne has crafted a collection of comfortable, yet sexy jumpsuits, dresses and knitwear.

WWW.HUNKON.COM

GRÓA

Hailing from Denmark, designer Gro Abrahamsson has spent the past few years developing her edgy but always super-feminine signature style, crafted in the finest fabrics. Contrasts lie at the heart of her philosophy: each collection is made up of distinctly individual pieces with their own unique expression.

WWW.GROA.DK

STEINUM

The Faroe Islands are home to more sheep than people and a strong knitting community. Johanna av Steinum was raised in this tradition, sitting on the laps of her seven knitting aunties. With a tongue-in-cheek wit her designs are steeped in the region's craftsmanship.

WWW.STEINUM.NET

YOUR FREE PASS
Admission to Cph Vision is free if you sign up before 31 January. During registration you will receive a PDF file with a QR-code, which will function as your pass at the entrance.
WWW.CPHVISION.DK

BRUNSWICKER

ART DIRECTION
& GRAPHIC DESIGN

Title: The Vision Paper
New Blood and Talent Focus
Firm: Brunswicker
Art Director: Mark Brunswicker
Designer: Mark Brunswicker
Client: Exhibition Professionals

Statement:

Art direction of the biannual newspaper aimed for fashion buyers and professionals attending Copenhagen Fashion Week and fashion fairs: CPH Vision and Terminal 2. Brunswicker was tasked with finding a balance with fashion's lavishness and the industry's professionalism.

WWW.CPHVISION.DK

OU

NES

SKOU

CHA MARIC

...REPRESENTED AT CPH VISION AND TERMINAL-2, ...CONTEST DESIGNERS' NEST. ...COPENHAGEN FASHION WEEK.

...represented at the different fashion fairs. Here you will find huge ...ands as well as up-and-coming independent designers. ...have an impressive schedule with more than 60 shows on the ...the fashion fairs – that's unique. It creates an intense Fashion Week, ...nd the press are assembled, all focused on making deals and ...nds. Plus Copenhagen is a great city for a Fashion Week; its ...ack.

...ES SCANDINAVIAN FASHION DESIGNERS SPECIAL? "I ...the casual and timeless approach to design. We also have many ...graduated designers, who have very little funding, showing ...k. That combination of talent and drive makes Scandinavian ...to beat."

...OURNALISTS, STYLISTS AND OPINION LEADERS FROM ...NK ABOUT SCANDINAVIAN DESIGN? "Many mention the talent ...region. That's also why it is so important to keep focusing on new ...can continue to deliver on new designers and brands. ...is that we are often described as being relaxed and playful. ...a long history for design and the good life in general – including ...furniture, contemporary art and gourmet food."

...VIEW CHANGED IN RECENT YEARS? "My impression is that ...to return season after season to enjoy Scandinavian lifestyle and ...ing new talent. They feel that a visit to Copenhagen Fashion Week. ...d inspiring."

...OU THINK ABOUT THE INCREASING COMPETITION ...OPENHAGEN AND OTHER FASHION CAPITALS? "Copenhagen ...we have proven that we have what it takes to be compared with huge ...erlin and London – that makes me proud. ...only city to discover the future of Scandinavian fashion."

...EVER WHEN A LONGHAIRED MAN OF DIMINUTIVE STATURE
...CED THE VERY FIRST COLLECTION OF HIS EPONYMOUS
...IONS THAT BOTH SHOCKED AND SURPRISED, THE LABEL –
...IONYMOUS WITH PIONEERING FASHION AND ZEITGEIST.

In keeping with the brand's international profile and philosophy to coexist with the modern urban individual, "Marc by Marc Jacobs is more than just quirky, trendy designs, quality leather and beautiful colours, it's also a lifestyle: a particularly experimental, creative and playful attitude to modern life," says Scandinavian PR & Communications Manager Asbjørn Riis-Søndergaard. "Marc Jacobs is an artist; fashion is meaningless alone and it is first when placed in a social context that it becomes exciting, inspiring and magical," he adds. The brand's profile is therefore to be interpreted and understood in relation to the local milieu and the cultural mechanisms that control daily life in the city the brand, "In our case, it's Scandinavia with boutiques in Copenhagen and Stockholm. We work with the distinctive preferences and behaviour patterns that exist in each city, taking these into account when we interpret the label Marc by Marc Jacobs," he adds.

Thus far in 2011, the team has married fashion's exclusivity with the urban subcultures in Copenhagen through initiatives such as Broken Hearts Club – the hyped Berlin club which transformed the city store to a heaving international nightclub. Other initiatives to unite the global with the local and highlight the international format of the brand's presence in the market include an in-store pop-up coffee lounge and whisky bar, a brand birthday bash at Copenhagen's trendy meat packing district. Marc's personal Guide to Copenhagen and summer BBQs in collaboration with the city's annual Distortion music festival. And during Copenhagen Fashion Week Marc by Marc Jacobs is cooperating with CPH Vision to focus on uniting the city's underground environment and elements of New Yorker-style street culture.

Later this year plans to further cement Marc by Marc Jacobs' philosophy in Scandinavia will be set in action through boutique birthday events, product launches and parties to unite the fashion elite with the subculture faction. "The Marc by Marc Jacobs universe is exclusive, luxurious and trendy and therefore appeals to urban men and women who are quality and style conscious, creative, edgy and brave at the same time. Since this perception of the brand is generally applicable worldwide, it's not so much about 'reinventing the brand', but more about inviting people to be a part of this exciting universe," Asbjørn Riis-Søndergaard concludes.

NOT JUST A LABEL IS EXACTLY THAT. LAUNCHED IN 2008 BY BROTHERS STEFAN AND DANIEL SIEGEL, NOT JUST A LABEL (NJAL) IS A WEB-BASED PLATFORM TO SUPPORT AND NURTURE EMERGING TALENT IN THE FASHION INDUSTRY. THE INNOVATIVE BRAND IS TODAY SYNONYMOUS WITH PROFILING CONTEMPORARY FASHION FROM UPCOMING DESIGNERS ACROSS THE GLOBE, AND IS A FRONTRUNNER IN DEMOCRATISING STYLE.

A TALENT FOR TALENT

The idea for Not Just a Label was born from the brothers' desire to use the internet as a fashion networking site. Specifically targeting graduate and avantgarde fashion designers, the website globally showcases their collections without the usual hurdles faced by upcoming designers.

Recognised by the industry as a one-stop shop for emerging talent, the site has become a staple with fashion editors and stylists scouting for the next big thing. The progressive website also lets consumers source information about and purchase design by the designers of tomorrow. In turn, the designers receive a free global forum from which they gain worldwide exposure to help build their brand. For some upcoming designers, Not Just a Label can mean international exposure in leading fashion magazines such as Vogue and Dazed & Confused.

Earlier this year NJAL celebrated its third birthday with the launch of a new website and online shop, offering a selection of designer clothes produced by more than 5,000 emerging talents from over 80 countries, and that is each month filled with new stock curated by some of fashion's leading insiders. The Vision Paper caught up with co-founder Stefan Siegel – one of this season's Designer's Nest judges – to talk about talent.

What, in your opinion, are the most important qualities an upcoming designer should possess?
"I am always fascinated by designers who lack their designs with a deep inspiration that reflects their personality or illustrates events in their life. When reading collection descriptions, much of the time, you feel like you have read it all before, and mostly it is written tell after the collection has been created, when a sales manager has to maximise sales and exposure. Real designers are independent; they design as a way to express themselves. You can really see this in their garments."

How can the industry best nurture new talent in the fast-moving realm of fashion?
"By taking the speed out of fashion! Individuality has become a statement for luxury. The appetite and demand for alternative and sustainable production is predominant

in many sectors such as food, hospitality, lifestyle and I hope fashion will be next. Young designers recognise their responsibility in creating sustainable fashion. We believe it is more valuable and eco-friendly to buy an item that will last for many seasons. By buying directly from a designer you support local production, local business and help a young creative talent. I think consumers have to do their part too!"

What are the greatest challenges new designers face, and how can they best overcome these?
"Since we have started Not Just A Label I feel the market has changed drastically; at the moment I believe there are more opportunities than challenges for young designers. However, designers have to be willing to be creative not only in terms of design, but also when planning their marketing and branding strategy, when selecting stockists and focusing on their regional markets. We live in a global market, which means designers have to be willing to leave antiquated methods behind and run their businesses on five continents at the same time. Opportunity and challenge in one, it just depends how you look at it."

If he, in your opinion, should we be keeping an eye on and why?
"Me when I start going out in Copenhagen! Jokes aside, we have been visiting Denmark for the last few seasons and the number of strong design talent is incredible. I really hope they will start to operate internationally very soon!"

Is there a country that is currently particularly good at producing new talent? And what do you think this can be attributed to?
"We have in more areas from seeing fashion as something which happens in four cities, or places famous for a school. In the past three years I have seen talented designers come from places I would have never imagined. The quality of design schools, as well as the access to production, is crucial. Countries like Indonesia, Brazil, Mexico and Latvia are surprising us every season. But furthermore, we were also able to scout fantastic designers from Poland, Lebanon, Ukraine and Slovenia. Overall, there is no longer a standard benchmark, we just have to accept creativity is now global and celebrate this as an opportunity for the fashion industry as a whole."

WWW.NOTJUSTALABEL.COM

THE
NEW
VISION

BRIDGING THE REALMS OF CREATIVITY AND COMMERCE

INTRODUCING
COPENHAGENS
NEW
FASHION
PLATFORM

VISION

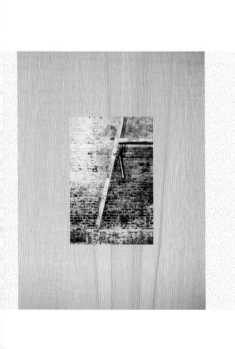

5243 20

Title: The New Vision
Firm: Brunswicker
Art Director: Mark Brunswicker
Designer: Mark Brunswicker
Client: Exhibition Professionals

Statement:

VISION is a biannual trade show based on an extended fusion of CPH Vision and Terminal 2 fashion fairs in Copenhagen.

Brunswicker Studio created the VISION concept in collaboration with Frederik Bjerregaard and Exhibition Professionals, and we did the overall branding consisting of a new logo, brand identity, stationery, concept paper, signage, and interior decorating.

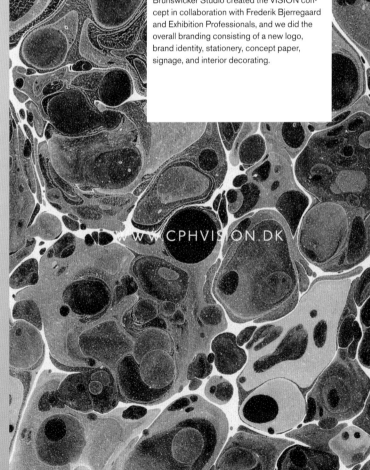

WWW.CPHVISION.DK

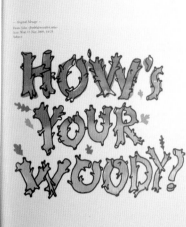

Title: Spam Jam
Firm: Bruketa & Žinić OM
Art Directors: Davor Bruketa, Nikola Žinić (Creative Directors); Nebojša Cvetkovi (Art Director, Illustrator, Designer)
Designer: Nebojša Cvetkovi
Other Credits: Toni Klarič (Copywriter), Vesna Đurašin (Production Manager), Ana Šutić (Account Executive), Marko Ostrež (DTP)
Client: Igepa group
Client Industry: Paper

Printer: Stega tisak
Paper: Igepa paper
Color: 4 color + Pantone 805 + UV varnish and foil

Illustrator: Nebojša Cvetkovi

Statement:

We have peeked into a forgotten junk mail folder and created a limited edition designers' picture book titled *Spam Jam* for Igepa, picturing a world we secretly yearn for. The book has fifty-two pages and it contains original illustrations. It is printed on Igepa paper and divided thematically into three parts: Spam Data, Spam Messages, and Spam Future.

Spam Data abounds with various, more or less well-known facts about what spam is and what it most often promotes, and it also includes some spam statistics. Spam Messages contains various representative spam messages and Spam Future wraps up the story with a futurist vision of spam seen by the authors of the book.

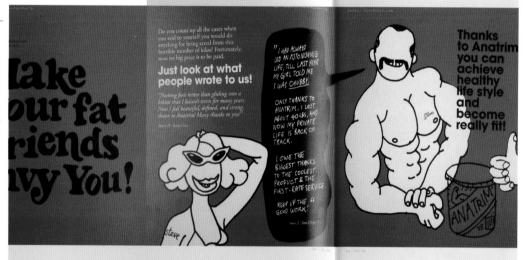

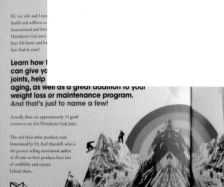

Title: Chiasso Letteraria, Per Mare
Firm: CCRZ
Art Director: Paolo Cavalli
Designer: Marco Cassino
Client: Festival Internazionale di Letteratura Chiasso

Printers: Salvioni Arti Grafiche (newspaper), Progetto Stampa, (others)
Methods: Rotary press (newspaper), Offset (brochure, postcard, program, pass)
Color: Fluorescent ink

Statement:

Prints for an International Festival of Literature

The body of a tabloid with the spirit of a magazine. Huge photography and lovely blue and black duotones work the space.

Centered type, blocked for readability?
Effortlessly cool.

Il mare é donna,
uomo é chi lo attraversa,
lo cavalca,
lo ama e lo teme.
Balena franca
http://chiassoletteraria.wordpress.com
post del 30/03/2011

Il Mare non può essere femminile.
E' troppo logico, spietato, curante soltanto di sé stesso.
Fornisce la vita a tutto e se la riprende quando vuole.
Si aizza soltanto quando è provocato e non perdona mai.
Capitano Bligh
http://chiassoletteraria.wordpress.com
post del 20/02/2011

Title: Chiasso Letteraria, Per Mare
Firm: CCRZ

Obviously, we're having a love affair with newsprint and the co-opting of the newspaper format. It's economical.

A switch in type orientation actually
encourages reading.

16 ways Inscape makes smart* work spaces.

1

We talk applications first, then products.
We collaborate with our clients to provide customized solutions based on their unique spaces and individual needs.

Title: Inscape applications brochure
Firm: Concrete Design Communications
Art Directors: Diti Katona, John Pylypczak
Designers: David Adams, Ty Whittington
Client: Inscape
Client Industry: Product/Manufacturing

Printer: Transcontinental PLM
Method: Offset
Colors: 4 color + 5-color process

3

We maximize your real estate. We've reduced vertical storage height and increased capacity by building in 1.5" increments. This gives you far more usable, flexible and accessible storage. And you can choose from 2,808 paint colors.

*Replace your lateral files containing 10" drawers with our laterals made up of 10½" drawers and you'll not only increase your storage space but you'll also gain increased access to the number of drawers within reach, from floor to five.

4

Our solutions can be easily and repeatedly reconfigured (yes, really) as staffing requirements change. This creates a true lower cost of ownership.

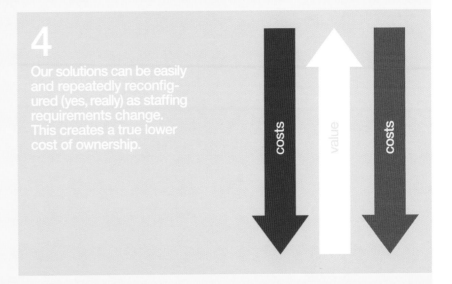

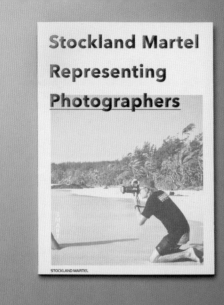

Title: Stockland Martel Representing
Photographers 2012
Firm: design MW
Client: Stockland Martel

Printer: GZD
Prepress: Shoot Digital

Photo Editor: Ekaterina Arsenieva
Staff Photos: Jeff Lipsky
Copy: Kristina Feliciano

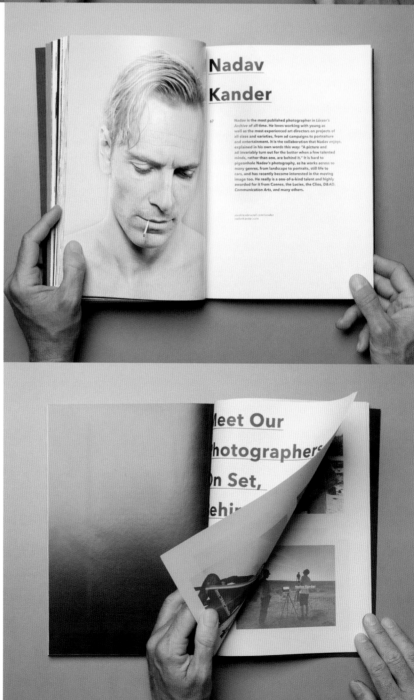

KWAKU ALSTON

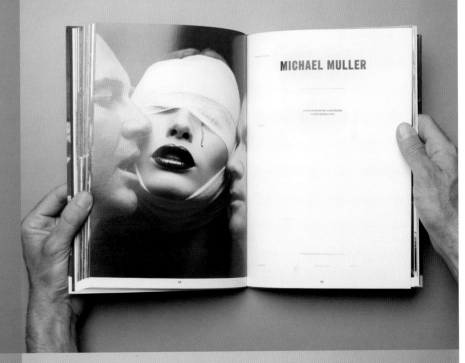

MICHAEL MULLER

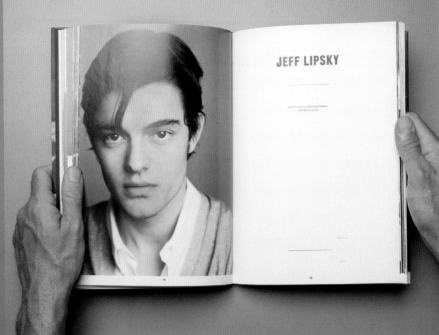

JEFF LIPSKY

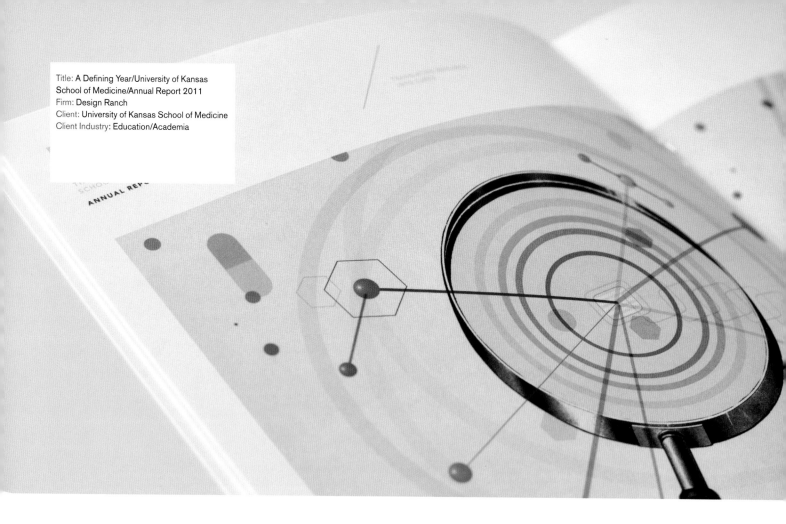

Title: A Defining Year/University of Kansas
School of Medicine/Annual Report 2011
Firm: Design Ranch
Client: University of Kansas School of Medicine
Client Industry: Education/Academia

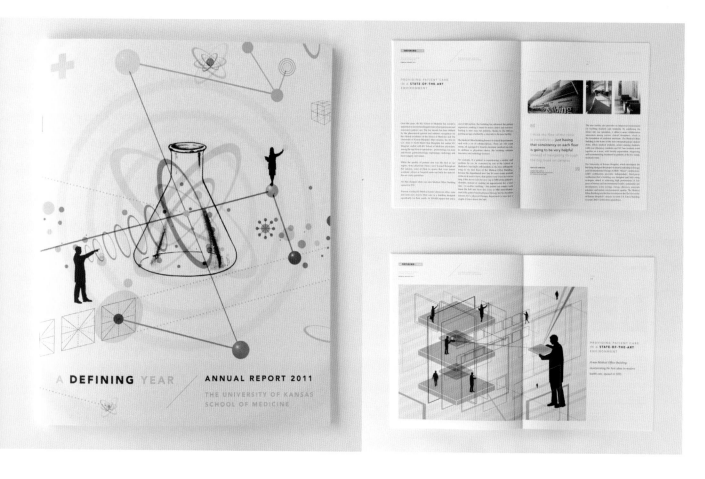

Title: KCAI National Portfolio Day
Firm: Design Ranch
Client: Kansas City Art Institute
Client Industry: Education/Academia

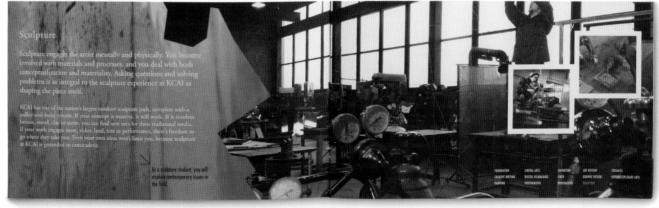

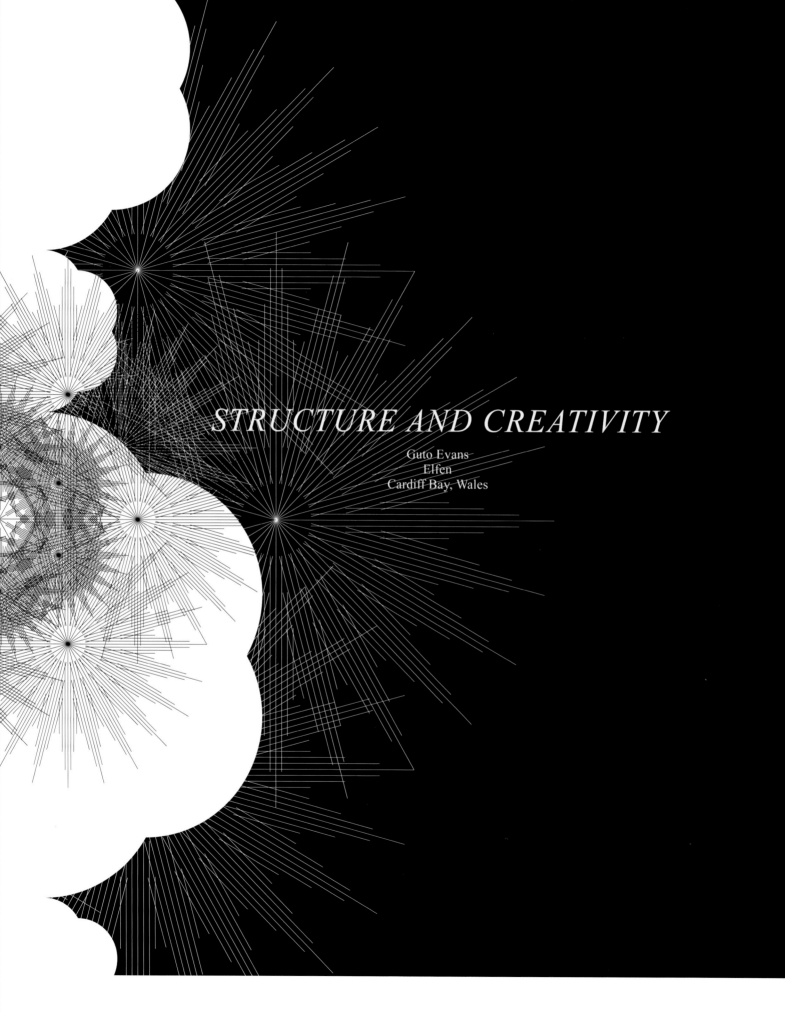

STRUCTURE AND CREATIVITY

Guto Evans
Elfen
Cardiff Bay, Wales

A brochure is just one output of a project. Rarely these days does Elfen get commissioned to design just a brochure, because its role has changed. For us, it is now part of the communication jigsaw; it needs to be special rather than mass produced.

For National Theatre Wales, each project has a brief that is part of the wider communications package for productions. We always start with the brief—what the particular director wants to communicate, and who the potential audiences are. Then we discuss what the communication package includes. There is always a different mix—online, offline and say, outdoor advertising, for example—which influences the creative direction.

As a studio, we collaborate heavily with our clients in the initial phases of a project. With National Theatre Wales, meeting directors and artists is a really important part of our process. We map their theories and ideas onto ours. This process allows us to immerse ourselves in ideas—to investigate with no preconception of what formats and visual directions to take. The creative direction is driven by collaboration, and creative production is part and parcel of the overall solution. We have a very robust process that allows a project to be realized on a practical level—particularly in regard to time and money—there is no point in having a great idea and selling it to the client if it's going to blow the budget!

Having prescribed phases for every project helps our clients—some may be inexperienced in commissioning design. Providing a structure to work within gives them confidence in our creative process. If you work with any company or supplier and they have all the processes in place it really helps, whether you're buying online, designing a garden, or getting a suit tailored. If I am getting my suit tailored, I want to know the cost, how many appointments I will need, what each one will be about, how long they will take, will I need to supply anything, and when will it be done.

So phases are mapped out for the client. Initially, we gather information via questioning them, which is followed up by a variety of workshops which map out thoughts and objectives. We then have ideation sessions where we share ideas and look at initial design directions. This is where we try to inspire the client with directions and options. In the case of brochure design, we look at lots of different influences with the client. Inspiration can come from anywhere—there are no rules. For example you can use a piece of furniture that folds really differently as inspiration for a brochure—it doesn't have to be print related. At Elfen, we continually research design and production methods, keeping libraries of different formats, materials, architecture and so forth, so that when we have sessions with clients we have lots that we are excited about to share and discuss.

Being creative within a budget is a key skill—it's not about wild ideas that are impossible or too costly to produce. To do this we need the knowledge and expertise of knowing how different production methods work. For example, anticipating how an inline varnish unit on a particular press offers a great opportunity. Asking do the stitches come in different colors, at the same cost? On smaller runs, paper costs per sheet are not such an issue, but on large runs, it can make or break a project. Knowing when a certain quantity makes one press more expensive than another is important, like when a large run could work on a web press. Familiarity with parent sheet and press sizes can maximze pagination and work to your benefit, giving clients extra space for design and content at no extra production cost.

The final phases of design are how our collaboration with our client and our expertise with production come together. The investment in the early stages always pays off when you get the brochures back from print. Small details, when they come together, really do make a difference. A brochure is a bespoke product, tailor-made for your client. With a lot of printers trying to standardize print, we need to try even harder to make the finished piece unique and well crafted.

Guto

Artlog: 2010–2011 Program Guide
Firm: Elfen
Client: National Theatre Wales
Client Industry: Performing arts

Statement:
We continued the theme of the newspaper format, and for this brochure we had information for the first year of production, but we didn't have specific images for each show. We asked each of the directors to collect three objects that they felt reflected their shows, and then we set out to shoot these in a studio over a three-day period. The front cover is a collection of all of the objects together, reflecting all of the shows.

Gloss paper used in a tabloid format with no stitching in the bindery.

What do you do when you have no assets to work with? Make something. This collection of props on shelving creates a fun quirky personality for the theatre.

nationaltheatrewales.org

Artlog: The Persians
Firm: Elfen
Client: National Theatre Wales
Client Industry: Arts/Culture

Statement:

The Persians is an example of how we develop
an individual look for each production. It was
based on a military camp in west Wales. The
format of the production is very different—the
audience is guided around the space with
military vehicles and you're almost a part of the
production. The direction for the brochure and
visual was developed in a series of meetings
with the director. We wanted a military feel with
map codes and diagrams, but used color to
take them out of context. The format is more
traditional, but small details such as black
stitching wires, and translucent pages with
portraits, added some unusual qualities.

MIKE PEARSON
KAITE O'REILLY

MIKE PEARSON / DIRECTOR

It is 472 BC. At the City Dionysia in Athens, Aeschylus presents The Persians as one in his trilogy of plays. Its subject is the destruction of Xerxes fleet at Salamis eight years earlier, a battle that he himself witnessed; so he had at Marathon ten years before that, when Xerxes's father Darius too was repulsed. Uniquely, he tells the story from the perspective of the defeated invaders – no Greeks are mentioned. The names and costumes reveal an exotic world – alien, fascinating, yet a real and present danger. It is a work of reportage and conjecture, of anticipation and consequence; a caution against reckless adventurism and hubris. And as revelation follows revelation, the only possible outcome is grief and chaos. And a small hope of reconciliation.

In performance, the masked thespian – still in noise and tell as a reminder of the city's ordeal – provide a backdrop, the bleachers on which the audience is seated may come from the timbers or wreckage Persian ships, the stage seeming from the captured royal tent. Aeschylus is innovative: he introduces more than one actor and passages of dialogue, ominously, the Chorus is under threat – its function gone, its long decline unmannered. And he includes a ghost!

The Persians will survive as the earliest recorded drama, the only Greek tragedy based on an historical event.

It is 2010 AD at a place for testing battlefield scenarios – of rehearsing urban warfare, of performances. The Persians now in the era of 24-hour news – of images of far-off people and places whose names barely register – and of constant movie aftermax and intrusion. In a village that appears half built, or already half decayed, with women and children out of sight, ...an uneasy assembly to celebrate the anticipated triumph of formidable force, overwhelming in size and strength. Victory is assured. But the mood is tense: register change and even the collapse of empire will follow failure – the only possible outcome, a reversion to barbarism and ritual dunking beneath the surface veneer.

A chance to locate the moot basic of dramas in a contemporary plane of conflict: a vile that is re-imagined daily – as a stand-in for somewhere else in the world – by those who inhabit it fleetingly, whose presence and passing haunts it, a sense of constant anxiety, where someone is always trying to kill you.

But it's too easy to read this juxtaposition as a direct allusion to current world events. Instead, an attempt to reveal the timeless nature of mounting human ambition – through the collision of ancient and modern, in the frictions between drama and site.

An opportunity to revisit practices whose time appeared to have passed – site-specific performances made especially for and within particular places, where architecture and environment play a key role in creating dramatic meanings. To work with old colleagues whose hard-won theatrical knowledge and experience is once more fore-grounded; and with new, in the creation of innovative approaches to production suited to the ambitions of a 21st century National theatre.

Returning an originary moment in the Western canon to the very birth of a new endeavour, perception from a time before nation, at a time when the very notion of nation is under pressure.

That in itself is surely a remarkable achievement!

What became apparent during my research was the sense of a long line of practitioners who had, over the ages, made 'their' version of this great classic, informed, if not provoked, by the age through which they lived. I read excerpts where the expressionist Persian force are reinterpreted as Hitler, Saddam Hussein, and Bush Senior and Junior. There was blood over land, blood over oil and a post-apocalyptic 22nd century version with blood over water. I read Victorian versions

KAITE O'REILLY / WRITER

How do you make a new version of the first extant play in the Western theatrical tradition, the World's oldest recorded script, initially produced in 472 BCE and written, in my opinion, by a maude?

Although I am not a linguist, and therefore unable to read the text in the Ancient Greek, through my class reading of 23 translations, made across three centuries, I like to think I caught a sense of the base line – the instigating 'moe' (Aeschylus, poet, philosopher, soldier-playwright), soil-warmonger, humanist, he close to write about an astonishing, almost miraculous event: the spectacular and relatively recent defeat of the marauding Persian Imperial force by the people of Athens at the Battle of Salamis. Aeschylus was an Athenian; he could have written a newspaper tale of victory, a xenophobic pageant of blood reet, filled with self-congratulation to Greek cunning and sacrifice to protect the emerging experiment in 'democracy'. Instead, he wrote a powerful anti-war play which painfully depicts the waste and agonies of conflict – the pity of war – written with this not dignity from the point of view of the defeated.

Aeschylus aside, this version was written with the knowledge of Mike Pearsons work since Gododdin in 1989. I feel immensely fortunate to have worked on this script, informed by the work of these two great practitioners, in what has been an illuminating and exhilarating project stiff with finesse and patrioms, indigestible poetry toreshadowing the death of Empire, and brown Modernist inter-war versions, debrying war whilst anticipating another. I began to pay attention to the year the translation was made in order to comprehend the socio-political Times in which it was written.

There was always something that warranted a new translation or production of this particular play – invariably the anticipation of, the participation in, the protesting against, or the recovery from a long, bloody, and in many cases, unnecessary conflict.

During my reading I was inexhaustibly aware of this rope of new versions reaching back to the first millennia BCE. It was strangely emotional to think that in my own small way I would be joining it.

There is a time, however, when the romance must stop and the effort goes into making a script which is playable – basically a piece of theatre which works. So how to proceed? I chose not to reinvent. I chose to be as faithful, as far as I could perceive it, to that initial 'moie' and to trust that the extraordinary location in which the performance takes place would create a context with more resonance than anything I could ever fabricate. The text is just one of many layers in Mike Pearson's production – there is choreography, the music by John Hardy, the fine work of the company, and, most significantly, the site itself.

Artlog: Perseverance
Firm: Foundry Communications
Art Director: Zahra Al-Harazi
Designer: Jake Lim
Client: Celtic Exploration Ltd.
Client Industry: Industry

Printer: Blanchette Press

Photographer: Colin Way
Writers: Jenny Allford, Sadiq Lalani

Statement:
We took infographics to a new level with the Celtic annual report. The overall theme was "defining Celtic." We wanted to keep it simple and minimalist, yet engaging and clever. We let the numbers speak for themselves and used two colors for the entire annual to ensure clarity and simplicity. The goal was to touch on Celtic's virtues of perseverance and patience and let the strengths of the company shine.

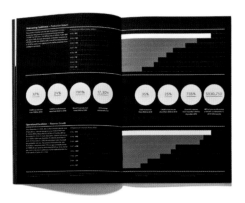

Artlog: 475
Firm: Graham Hanson Design
Art Director: Graham Hanson
Designer: Lydia Stone
Client: Cohen Brothers Realty Corporation
Client Industry: Real Estate

Title: Humus
Firm: Humus Design
Art Director: Massimiliano Sagrati
Designer: Alfredo Laneve
Client: Humus Design
Client Industry: Graphic Design
(self-promotion)

Papers: Gmund, Munken

Photographer: Stefano Compagnucci

Statement:

The notebook has been realized with the aim
of communicating the origin of our design
studio and the reason behind the company
name (humus is the organic matter which
fertilizes the soil and promotes growth). It is
given to the clients, suppliers, and friends
to use throughout the year to take down
work-related notes, thoughts, and ideas.
The notebook is enriched with photographs
taken by Stefano Compagnucci: close-ups
of different leaves that also resemble satellite
images of towns. The work has been realized
using paper, printing techniques, and staging,
which continue the theme of nature that the
whole concept aims to emphasize.

Title: Ossigeno
Firm: Humus Design
Art Director: Massimiliano Sagrati
Designer: Emanuela Cappelli
Client: Ottavio Celestino
Client Industry: Photography (self-promotion)

Papers: Fedrigoni Imitlin Aida,
Fedrigoni Arcoprint

Statement:

Ottavio Celestino is a Rome-based photographer who specializes in fashion, portraits and has always been involved in several artistic projects. His book entitled Ossigeno is a tale of many parts in which both commercial and research-based photography find their ground. His work can be disturbing as well as satisfying; it has a dual nature shared with oxygen, and it is necessary like oxygen. The graphic concept echoes the chemical structure of the elements and their concise representation. The symbol for oxygen is O (also the initial of the photographer) and its corresponding number in the periodic table is 8 (that is "Otto" in Italian which is also the photographer's nickname).

Artlog: Les Canaux de la Mode 2011
Firm: Mainstudio
Art Director: Edwin van Gelder
Client: Orang'Frog Event Production
Client Industry: Fashion

Paper: Wegener Newsprint

Photographer: Wendelien Daan

Statement:

Les Canaux de la Mode is an international platform for networking and cocreation, connecting Dutch fashion designers and French couture craftsmen on both creative and business levels. Mainstudio designed the publication that accompanies Les Canaux de la Mode's exhibitions in Paris (July 2011) and Amsterdam (November 2011).

The design of this publication is that of an inverted newspaper. The inside pages are the cover and backpage, and vice versa. The publication can be approached from two sides: starting with the end results—the final cocreations made by the craftsmen and fashion designers—or with the proces. The raspberry cover is a reference to the same colored curtain that hangs in the actual exhibition, separating the ateliers—process—and the exhibition—results.

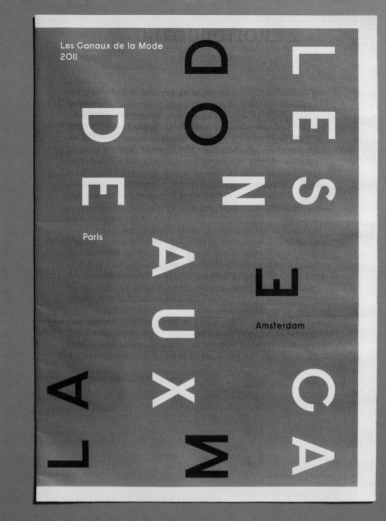

CAPE

LES CANAUX DE LA MODE

COLOPHON

PROJECT TEAM

Project management
  Céline Charlot
Board Members
  Nannet van der Kleijn
  Piet Paris
Communication & press NL
  Jan Schoon
Text writing
  Marie Bedrune
Press FR
  Les Ateliers de Paris/
  Clementine Michaud
Production
  Mariel Vieira
Assistants
  Stephanie Roblès
  Flore Vollard
  Laurette Veurmelen
Fundraising
  Carmen van Munnick
Styling and concept exhibitions
  And Beyond
  assistant Ilse Oosterhoff
Video production
  Sabine Morandini/
  Fascineshion

CATALOGUE

Graphic design
  Mainstudio/
  Edwin van Gelder
Printer
  Wegener Nieuwsdruk
Photography
  Wendelien Daan
Photography assistant
  Marloes van der Sloot
Hair
  Ingrid van Hemert/
  House of Orange
Make-up
  Liselotte van Saarloos/
  House of Orange
Model
  Eline van Houten/
  Code Management
Portrait & documentary
photography
  Anne-Marieke Hana
  Jeanpipol
  Jean-Paul Loyer
  Laetitia Schlumberger
  Nicole Roca
  Severina Lartigue
  Marga Weimans
  Céline Charlot

Thank You
  Isrid van Geuns
  Françoise Seince
  Valerie Antraigue/
  Les Ateliers de Paris
  Tonko Grever/
  Van Loon Museum
  Antoine Achten/
  Cultuur-Ondernemen
  Paulijn van der Pot
  Menno Born/
  Hermès Amsterdam
  Maarten Buursen/
  Mannequins Company
  Rob van Schaik
  Jaspar Roos
  Delphine Yague
  Josiane Cristofoli
  Nanda van der Berg
  Dorothée van hooft
  Ninke Bloemberg/
  Centraal Museum Utrecht
  Francine Pairon
  Lucas Delattre/
  IFM
  Alexandra Fau
  Daniel Wolf

Egbert van Gharldorp
Eva Olde Monnikhof
Han Grooten Feld
Marc Kwakman
Charlotte Franco
Manon Steglitz
Nanja Grooterman
Macarena Mendoza
Stephanie Moulin
Emmanuelle
Grandjean
Aude Medori
Stephanie Perez
Jasper van der Vorst
Sophie & Christian

F BKVB

AIM Amsterdam Innovation Motor

Gemeente Amsterdam
Stadsdeel Centrum

Royaume des Pays-Bas

MAIRIE DE PARIS

CLIFFORD CHANCE

With the kind support of
Kairos Co

MAISON DESCARTES

MANNEQUIN COMPANY

LES
ATELIERS
DE PARIS

FASHION
CRAFTS

2011

LES CANAUX DE LA MODE

Title: A New Concept in the Diagnosis of
Skin Diseases
Firm: Marius Fahrner Design
Art Directors: Marius Fahrner,
Falco Hannemann
Designer: Falco Hannemann
Client: Dermatology Diagnostics
Client Industry: Medical Science

Printer: Werbe- und Sofortdruck,
Leipzig (Germany)
Method: Offset
Colors: 4 color + 1 color, matte lamination,
partial gloss varnish (cover)

Photographer: Martin Zitzlaff

Title: Günther Franke Gruber
Firm: Marius Fahrner Design
Art Director: Marius Fahrner
Designers: Christian Tönsmann, Marius Fahrner
Client: GFG – Günther Franke Gruber,
Developers
Client Industry: Real Estate

Printer: RESET, Hamburg (Germany)
Method: Offset
Colors: 4 color + 2 color, hotfoil silver

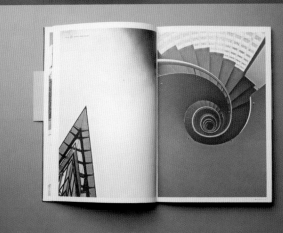

Title: Exhibition zines
Impressions from South Africa + German
Expressionism; Sanja Ivekovic; Taryn Simon;
Diego Rivera
Firm: Department of Advertising and
Graphic Design, The Museum of Modern Art
Creative Director: Julia Hoffmann
Production Manager: Claire Corey
Designer: Jesse Reed
Client: The Museum of Modern Art
Client Industry: Arts/Culture

Printer: Expedi Printing
Method: Offset
Color: 4 color

Title: you build buildings. we build confidence.
+ developing expertise. building careers.
Firm: Mende Design
Art Director: Jeremy Mende
Client: Davis Langdon

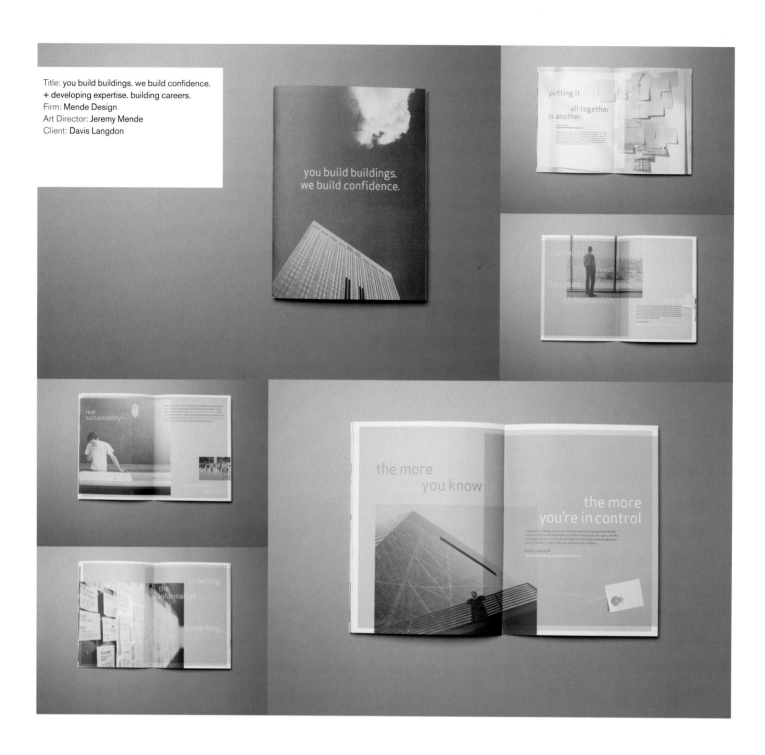

Artlog: Resin catalogs
Firm: Nothing Something New York
Client: Resin
Client Industry: Fashion

Title: Design Your Floor!
Firm: Peopledesign
Art Director: Yang Kim
Designers: Michele Brautnick, Gina Caratelli,
Adam Rice
Client: Interface
Client Industry: Product/Manufacturing

Printer: MPS
Method: Lithography
Paper: Mohawk

Font: Franklin Gothic
Photographer: Mitch Ranger
Writer: Peopledesign

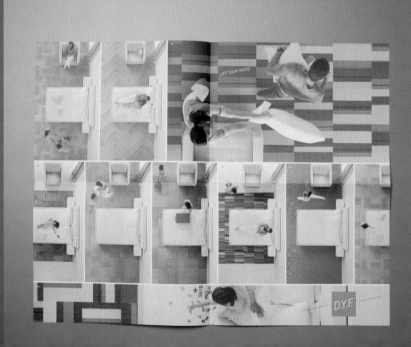

Title: Craft Print
Firm: Splash Productions Pte Ltd
Art Director: Stanley Yap
Designer: Stanley Yap
Client: Craft Print Ltd
Client Industry: Printing

Photographer: Stanley Yap
Writer: Michelle Fun

Statement:
Craft Print wants to display the texturing capabilities of its newest printer, so we've designed a brochure that showcases skill and feel. It flaunts the varnishing, metallic, and textural effects that Craft Print's new machine can print on a single surface in a single run. Who needs luck when you've got the best people and technology?

THE WINNING HAND IS HARDLY A GAMBLE. IT IS SKILL AND EXPERIENCE, TWO THINGS CRAFT PRINT HAS AND IS PROUD TO SHARE. PRINTING HAS BEEN OUR BUSINESS FOR OVER 35 YEARS, AND WE HAVE RECEIVED MANY AWARDS ALONG THE WAY. GET ACCESS TO A FULL HAND OF PRINTING POSSIBILITIES CREATED BY PASSIONATE PRINT EXPERTS.

WE OFFER A FULL SUIT CENTERED AROUND YOUR PRINTING NEEDS. YOU COULD MIX COLOR AND TEXTURE GRADIENTS OR MATCH A GLOSSY VARNISH WITH A FOIL STAMP. A PRINT SPEAKS AS MUCH AS THE CONTENT IT DELIVERS, AND WE'LL GIVE WHAT IT TAKES TO CREATE A WINNING COMBINATION.

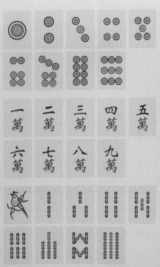

Three words: Insanely glossy paper. It's so wonderfully funky and pefectly graphic.

Title: Thieves
Firm: The White Room Inc.
Art Director: Karolina Loboda
Designer: Karolina Loboda
Client: Sonja den Elzen
Client Industry: Fashion

Printer: Colour Innovations
Method: Offset
Papers: Neenah Environment PC 100 White, 80 C Smooth Finish, 100% Post Consumer Fibre
Color: 4-color process

Fonts: Archer, Leitura, Pomegranate
Photographer: Maxime Bocken
Beauty: Kevin Smith
Models: Elise Helene, Elmer Olsen
Styling: Christina Viera

Statement:

The brochure was created to promote Thieves latest Autumn/Winter 2009 collection.

Founded in 2006 by Sonja den Elzen, Thieves was born out of her desire to harmonize her ethical commitments to sustainability with her passion for design.

Thieves uses sustainable fabrics such as hemp blends, peace silks, organic wools, organic cottons, lyocell, vegetable tanned leather, recycled materials, organic linen, bamboo, and soy. All pieces are conceived and assembled in Toronto.

The softness of the images and design speaks to the natural self-expression and high-end fashion that is Thieves.

Title: Global Review 2011
Firm: Studio 2br
Art Director: David Shalam
Designer: Dave Young
Client: Ernst & Young
Client Industry: Financial Services

Printer: Push
Method: Litho
Papers: FSC silk 250 gsm + super matte
laminate (cover), GF Smith PhoeniXmotion
135 gsm (text)
Colors: 4-color process + 2 PMS + spot
machine varnish

Fonts: EYInterstate
Photographers: Michael Fair, John Wildgoose

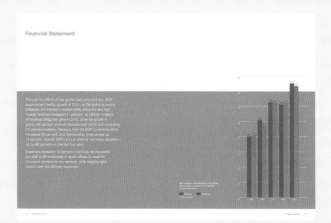

Title: Redefining Leadership
Firm: Tomorrow Partners
Art Director: Gaby Brink
Designer: Alex Styc
Client: BSR (formerly Business for Social Responsibility)

Printer: Hemlock Printers
Paper: Mohawk Loop

Photographers: Daria Hueske, Louis Vest, Christopher Herwic, Margarita Azucar, Nick Borzo, Marc Lewkowitz, David J. Green
Illustrator: Alex Styc
Writers: BSR staff

Statement:

BSR, formerly Business for Social Responsibility, is a nonprofit corporate responsibility consultancy that leverages its global network to develop sustainable solutions with leaders of every industry. As its agency of record, we have helped them develop a brand that brings their inspiring mission—"We work with business to create a just and sustainable world"—to light with a greater sense of purpose, optimism, action, and impact. The annual report allows BSR to maintain transparency, analyze trends, and establish its thought leadership. Documentary-style photography of BSR consultants in the field highlights their work from board room to factory floor, while carefully selected info graphics help their impact pop off the page.

Title: Taking the Guilt Out of Paper
Firm: VSA Partners, Inc.
Designers: Brandt Brinkerhoff,
Katherine Walker
Client: Sappi Fine Paper North America
Client Industry: Paper/Print

Printer: Lake County Press (LCP)
Method: Offset UV
Papers: Opus Dull 100 lb/148 gsm (text),
Opus Dull 100lb/270 gsm (cover)
Color: 4-color process, match green touch
plate plus spot dull reticulating UV varnish and
overall UV satin coating with dry trap triple hit
spot soft touch UV.

Photographers: Tom Maday (tommaday.com),
Mark Smalling (VSA in-house photographer)
& iStock Photo
Illustrator: Lauren Nassef (laurennassef.com)
Writer: Stephen Camelio (stephencamelio.com)

Statement:

As an industry leader with years of field experience and technical knowledge, we know it is our duty to show how sustainable forestry results in healthier forests and thriving wildlife. Fourth in the series, this volume begins to unravel the myths about paper, taking the guilt out of paper. Included in the piece is a series of positive statement stickers and a profile of Hans Wegner, National Geographic Society.

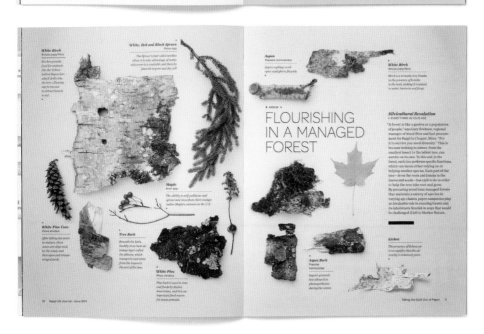

Title: Feel Every Note
Firm: WAX
Creative Director: Joe Hospodarec
Design Director: Monique Gamache
Designer: Hans Thiessen
Client: Victoria Symphony

Printer: Blanchette Press

Illustrator: Raymond Biesinger
Writer: Bethany Wilson
Account Manager: Maddie Gauthier
Production Manager: Kelly Sembinelli

* OUR 8,000M PEAK LEADERS ARE
SOME OF THE FINEST AND MOST
EXPERIENCED IN THE WORLD.
*SEE PAGE 88 FOR A SELECTION OF
OUR EXCEPTIONAL LEADERS.*

THE 8,000M PEAKS

Expeditions to the world's highest mountains

Jagged Globe 8,000m peak expeditions are among the best in the world: resourced and supported for reaching the summit.

Personally, we have been climbing 8,000m peaks for over 20 years, before the inception of professionally-led and guided expeditions to the Giants of the Himalaya. We used what we learnt on those mountains to launch the very first of our 8,000m peak expeditions and, as a professional organiser, by the mid 1990's we had climbed Broad Peak, Gasherbrum II, Cho Oyu, Shishapangma as well as Everest from both sides (north and south).

* We were the *first* British operator to climb Everest, and in 2009, continuing in the same vein, our team became the *first* British-organised team to climb the North East Face of Manaslu, placing the *first* British Woman, the *first* American Woman and the *first* New Zealander on one of its summits. In spring 2011, we are organising an expedition to the North side of Makalu, the world's 5th highest mountain. Again, this is a *first* for a British company. You can follow our team's progress via our website jagged-globe.co.uk.

Our huge experience of 8,000m climbing has enabled us to evolve the support and resources we bring to bear. Over two decades, we have refined our knowledge of how best to get each team member to the top of each mountain. Climbing at such enormous altitudes is not safe, and the risks involved are significant. We know the level of personal commitment it takes to climb: physically, mentally and emotionally. You won't find any corners cut, nor compromises contemplated, and no expedition resourced better than ours.

We will supply you with everything you need to at least match your expectations and aspirations.

Tim Rooth on the summit of
Everest, 23 May 2010. Details
of our Everest expedition are
on page 12.
© Elliot Anderson

/20

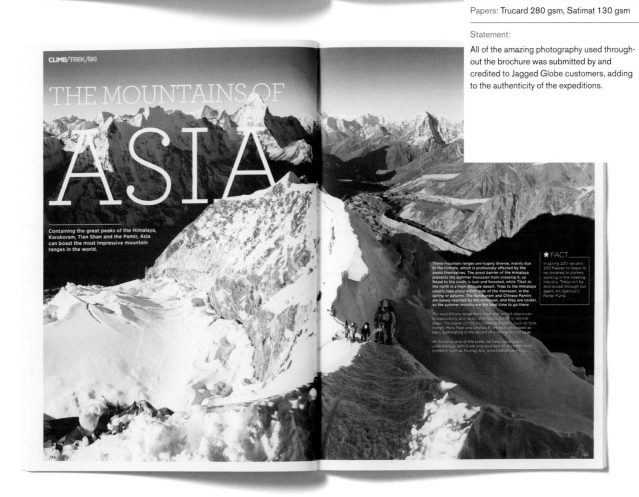

THE MOUNTAINS OF ASIA

Containing the great peaks of the Himalaya, Karakoram, Tien Shan and the Pamir, Asia can boast the most impressive mountain ranges in the world.

These mountain ranges are hugely diverse, mainly due to the climate, which is profoundly affected by the peaks themselves. The great barrier of the Himalaya prevents the summer monsoon from crossing it, so Nepal to the south is lush and forested, while Tibet to the north is a high-altitude desert. Trips to the Himalaya usually take place either side of the monsoon, in the spring or autumn. The Karakoram and Chinese Pamirs are barely reached by the monsoon, and they are colder, so the summer months are the best time to go there.

Our expeditions range from tried and tested objectives to exploratory and rarely attempted climbs in remote areas. The easier climbs on Trekking Peaks, such as Stok Kangri, Mera Peak and Lhakpa Ri are best described as treks culminating in the ascent of a non-technical peak.

At the other end of the scale, we have some major undertakings, which are only available to accomplished climbers, such as Muztag Ata, Ama Dablam and Nun.

* FACT ___
In spring 2011 we sent 200 fleeces to Nepal to be donated to porters working in the trekking industry. These will be distributed through our agent, Kit Spencer's Porter Fund.

/24   /25

Title: **Climb**
Firm: **We Are**
Designer: **Yvette Nuttall**
Client: **Jagged Globe**
Client Industry: **Adventure/Expedition**

Papers: **Trucard 280 gsm, Satimat 130 gsm**

Statement:

All of the amazing photography used throughout the brochure was submitted by and credited to Jagged Globe customers, adding to the authenticity of the expeditions.

Title: You Don't Know Anything About This
Firm: Zync
Client: Fragile X Research Foundation
of Canada

You don't
know anything
about this.

You don't know anything about this—
both a challenge and an invitation.

The running text continues to set Fragile
X Syndrome apart as something we can't
fit into our realm of experience, despite its
prevalence and commonality.

The photography depicting people going
about their lives—from a city to crowds to
just a silhouette of someone—suggests
an underlying and uncomfortable danger,
something looming all around us, getting
closer and more personal.

Quite a call to action.

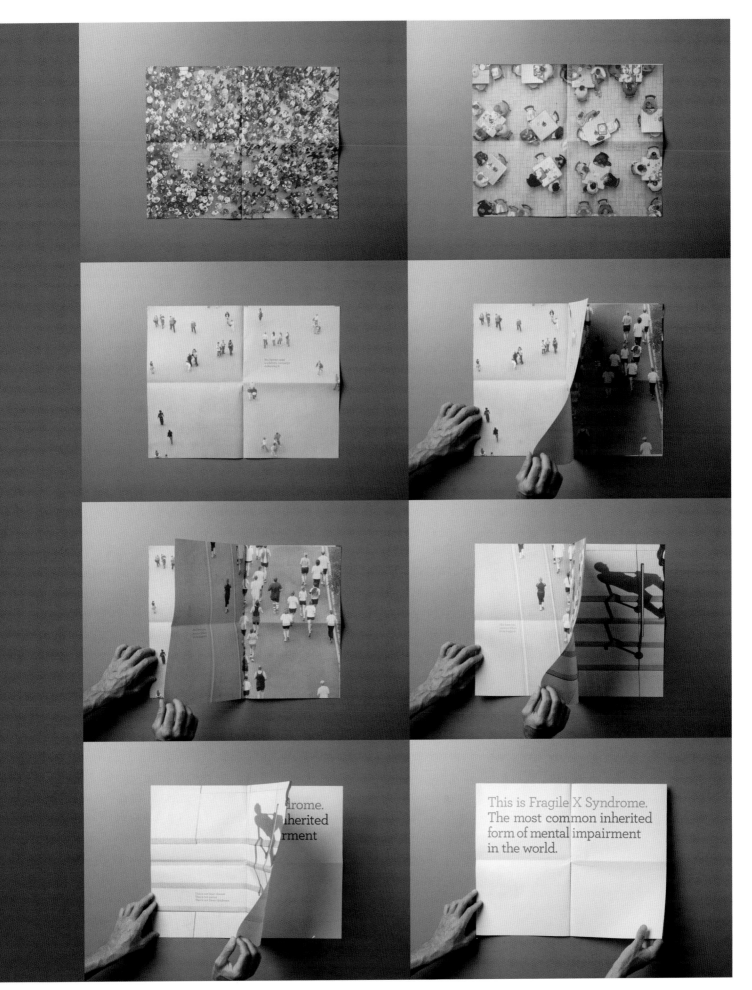

extra large

Title: Lida Baday/Fall/Winter 2011
Firm: Concrete Design Communications
Art Directors: Diti Katona, John Pylypczak
Designers: Melatan Riden, Leticia Luna
Client: Lida Baday
Client Industry: Fashion

Printer: Transcontinental PLM
Method: Offset
Color: 4 color

Photographer: Chris Nicholls

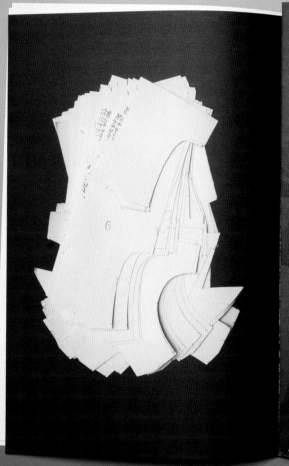

Title: Lida Baday/Fall/Winter 2011
Firm: Concrete Design Communications

Title: National Theatre Wales
Firm: Elfen
Client: National Theatre Wales

Statement:

For the launch brochure we didn't have any content to work with because the theater hadn't decided on any productions. The only thing we had was its manifesto—what it was going to set out to do. The creative process for the brochure was based around a photographic trip around locations in Wales to show the landscapes. We wanted a format that accentuated the landscapes. The resulting format is like a broadsheet newspaper. It can be taken apart and used as a poster.

'...it's not nat r
or our thond w
but the sh they
against the of ot

Owen Sheers
From 'Shadow Man'

ATRE WALES
SPOND

s full of company,
the birth of a star.
vider way to see.

ut their chemistry
nich our bodies bear.
it's full of company.'

Title: Music Friday
Firm: Go Welsh
Art Director: Craig Welsh
Designer: Scott Marz
Client: Music For Everyone/Lancaster, PA
Client Industry: Arts/Culture

Printer: Engle Printing
Method: Web
Paper: 50 lb Offset Newsprint

Statement:

This sixteen-page publication used to highlight
the city of Lancaster's free summer Music
Friday concert series and the first annual "Keys
for the City" public street piano project.

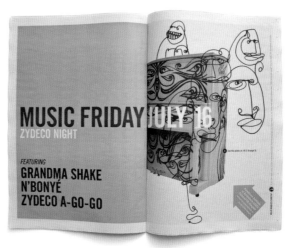

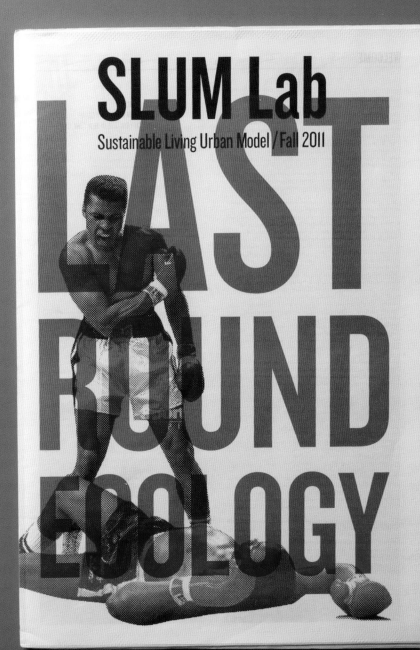

SLUM Lab

Sustainable Living Urban Model / Fall 2011

LAST ROUND ECOLOGY

Title: SLUM Lab
Firm: Paperwhite Studio
Art Director: Isaac Gertman
Client: Variance Objects
Client Industry: Fashion

Printer: J.S. McCarthy Printers
Method: Offset Lithography
Colors: 4-color process + soft touch varnish

Photographer: Molly DeCoudreaux

Statement:

S.L.U.M. Lab (Sustainable Living Urban Model) is a one hundred-page, large-format newsprint publication that brings the perspectives of urban planners, architects, and students from all over the world together to work toward an understanding of the link between urban planning, ecology, and poverty alleviation.

MEREDITH KAHN PRESENTS

MADE HER THINK

VOL UME XI

Title: Made Her Think Volume XI
Firm: Nothing Something New York
Client: Nothing Something New York

HAND
BAGS

RIGHT. RHINESTONE MAFIA

WRISTLET Measures 2" with Swarovski Rhinestones
Avail: Brass Ox with Smokey Quartz and Silver Ox with Crystal

Montana Blue

Title: Cassa NY Luxury Condominium
Firm: Graham Hanson Design
Art Director: Graham Hanson
Designer: Dorothy Lin
Client: Assa Properties
Client Industry: Real Estate

Material: Plexi Cover
Method: Silkscreen

210

Title: R3/LIFECYCLE / Volume 2
Firm: R3 Lab / R3lab.org
Art Director: Tom Sieu
Designers: Andrew Johnson, Jup Tummanon,
Shani Lyon, Lauren Forbes, Erik Carnes,
Rodrigo Zapata, Cristina Rotundo
Client: Academy of Art University, R3 Lab
Client Industry: Education/Academia

Printer: John Roberts Company
Method: UV Stochastic
Paper: French Durotone Butcher Extra White
100% PCW
Color: 4-color process + 1 PMS
Production notes: Entire piece was printed from
leftover make-ready sheets on the press floor.

Writers: Introduction by Phil Hamlett. Each
book is authored by respective designer. Each
designer was responsible for written content
as well as associated photography and/or
illustration.

Statement:

R3 Lab is a collaborative effort by the Academy
of Art University's graphic design students
and faculty to promote social and sustainable
design. Often, I get comments on the first day
of class from students about wanting to learn a
particular style. I find this quite disturbing when
they don't even know what the assignment is.
What we do is go beyond the framework of
just a designer's eye. We evaluate each project
as the maker, the marketer, the end-user. This
helps to provide a complete life-cycle analysis,
or the "complete experience." Then we are
designing something that has longevity and
staying power. Our roles are changing and we
need to adapt. If we give young designers the
permission, they can do amazing things.

This would be sophisticated thinking,
far-out and far-reaching, coming from any
Silicon Valley think tank, but it's students,
graphic design students, who are blowing
our minds. "A holistic approach to designing
better products" is both a study in how
graphic designers reach beyond print, as
well as how they use graphic design and
print to present and sell ideas that can
change everything.

FROM BRAZIL

TO MUMBAI

TODAY'S MODERN WORLD FACES AN EVEN TOUGHER GOAL. GLOBALIZATION, INCREASED POVERTY, AND ENERGY WASTE CONTINUE TO AFFECT BILLIONS OF PEOPLE AT AN ALARMING RATE.

$$E_k = \frac{1}{2}mv^2$$

Measure of kinetic energy

WHAT IF WE COULD CREATE RENEWABLE ENERGY WITH A SOCCER BALL. IMAGINE POWERING A COMMUNITY THROUGH A SINGLE GAME.

HUMANITY

NEEDS A STABLE SOLUTION

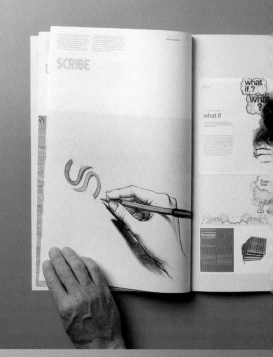

what if?
what if

Recycling one can reduces 95% of energy needed to produce a new one.

Title: R3/LIFECYCLE / Volume 2
Firm: R3 Lab / R3lab.org

It's funny that we have a brochure
of different books in this book
of different brochures.

Examples of better products as envisioned
by R3 Lab:

A soccer ball as a renewable energy source.

A reuseable ink-cartridge system.

A self-cooling 100% recycled aluminum can.

A line of recycled plastic bag clothing.

Plus, evocative photography, ecclectic
typography, graphic texture and pattern.
Fresh.

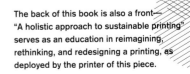

The back of this book is also a front—
"A holistic approach to sustainable printing"
serves as an education in reimagining,
rethinking, and redesigning a printing, as
deployed by the printer of this piece.

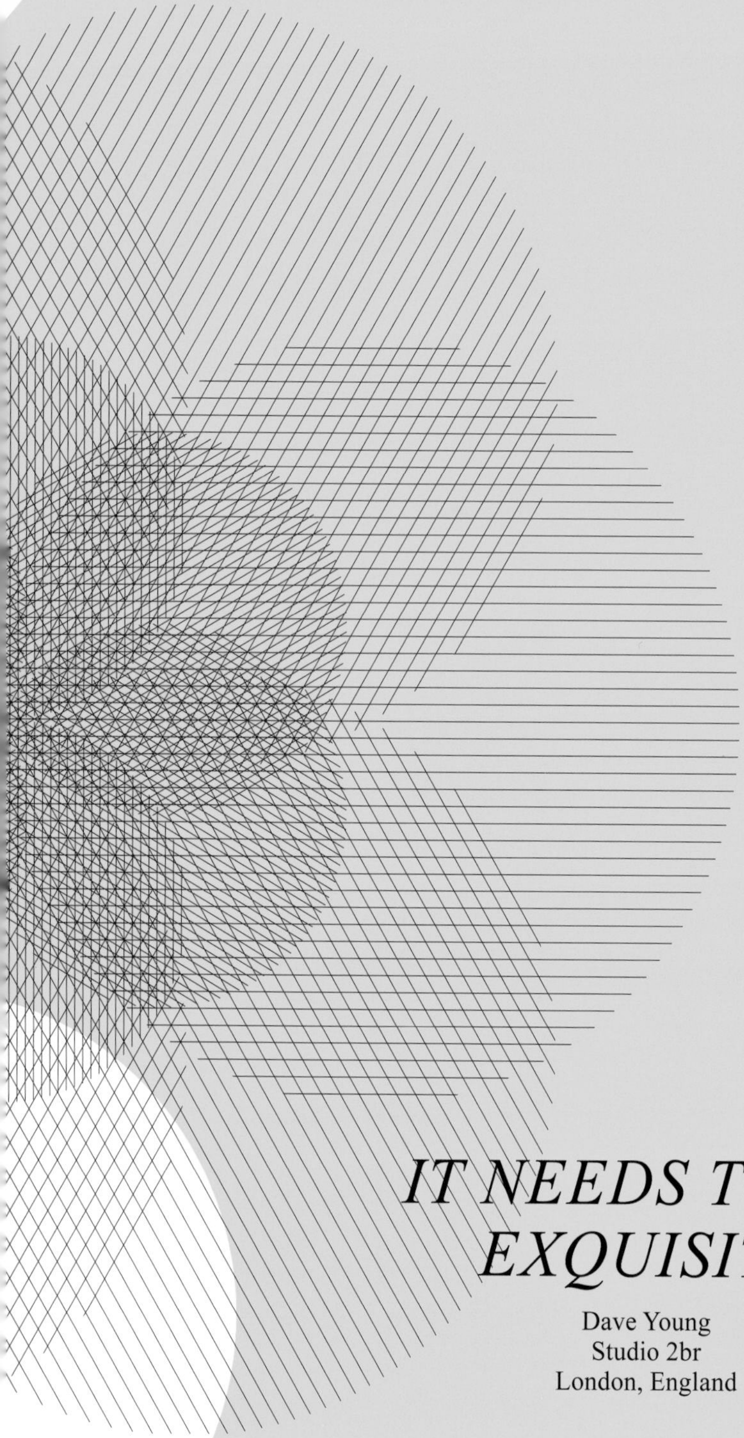

IT NEEDS TO BE EXQUISITE

Dave Young
Studio 2br
London, England

Studio 2br aims to provide large organizations with a clear-thinking, plain-speaking graphic design craft. We're passionate about print and naturally attracted to the processes involved in literature design. Of course we recognize that digital and print media must coexist today: All three projects submitted for this book exist online as microsites and in PDF format. Even so, there's still nothing designers like more than the smell of ink in the morning.

The growth of digital media only helps to reinforce our belief that if you're going to create a piece for print, it needs to be exquisite. This is not to say every project needs to be printed in twelve colors, foiled at Hogwarts, and thread-sewn by elves. Some of the work we're most proud of is straightforward four-color work on newsprint. But attention to detail is key: anything from making sure the fit on the last press pass is perfect at 2:00 a.m. on a Saturday morning, to rewriting a paragraph several times to lose that awkward widow. Details like this make all the difference.

The strength of print is that you can have sensory attributes—texture, weight, the rattle of paper, even the smell. We aim to capitalize on these qualities. For example, for this year's Ernst & Young Global Review, we used a super matte laminate on the cover not only to make the document durable and seal the ink, but also to give it a finish that feels soft and almost seductive to the touch. Spot matte and gloss varnishes on images and information graphics elevate the overall look and feel of the brochure, and in turn enhance the strength of the communication.

Asking questions

Over the years we've found that the corporate world often seems to lack the sophisticated approach to design found in the retail world. We see no reason why companies in the financial sector can't present themselves with the confidence of a retail brand from an aesthetic point of view, but also through the quality of the writing.

Writing is an essential part of our process and something that influences all our designs. An example of this approach can be found in our *Give & Go* project for Deutsche Bank. The client wanted to communicate the wide range of opportunities available to employees to take part in corporate citizenship-related activities—from volunteering and charitable giving to exhibitions and events at galleries and museums. We created Give & Go as an overarching theme

to promote any citizenship-related project or event, using familiar language to convey accessibility.

We approach each project by asking what the client is trying to achieve and who the client is trying to communicate with. If you have clear answers to these questions, you're halfway there before you've even begun.

Unexpected answers

Doing the unexpected can transform how a brand is perceived, and this is an area where corporations can learn a lot from how retail brands communicate and package their products. When Deutsche Bank wanted a brochure to celebrate the launch of a new permanent exhibition—the BrandSpace at its Frankfurt headquarters—we helped create something as out of the ordinary as the experience the bank had created.

The BrandSpace is built around dramatic, anamorphic interior design and lighting and innovative touch-screen technology. Reproducing the architecture's sense of changing perspectives in print involved a unique approach to photography called panography, a collage of photos that capture the anamorphic concept. The format of the brochure was inspired by the scale of the space. Producing a piece of print that, when opened, would have a flat size of 26.6 x 37.6 inches (677 x 956 mm) seemed an appropriate way to replicate the BrandSpace experience. Lastly, the brochure needed to be mailed to an influential audience, so we packaged it in a clay-coated, fluted board box that was screen printed with one of the 3D logos we designed for the bank.

Long live the brochure

Our love for the printed piece is enduring and is clearly shared by the other designers who have contributed to this book. Books like this are a great homage to the humble brochure. Even without some of the bells and whistles of print's digital mistress, we believe their relevance is as important as ever.

Dave

Title: The BrandSpace/Passion to Perform
Firm: Studio 2br
Creative Director: David Shalam
Designers: Dave Young, Daniel Hayes
Client: Deutsche Bank
Client Industry: Financial services

Printer: Westerham Press
Method: Litho + screen print
Papers: Fenner Paper Marazion 90 gsm and
1.25 white E-flute
Colors: 4-color process + 2-PMS and
screen printed 2 PMS

Font: Univers, Deutsche Bank
Photographers: Mareen Fischinger,
John Wildgoose, Nick David
Writer: Stuart Daniel

An assuming format, loose sheets
folded together, but overwhelming in scale—
the largest submission in this book

Of course, it's not the size, but what you do with it—minimal and concise text with larger-than-life photography that conveys the BrandSpace experience and Deutsche Bank brand messaging.

Title: swissnex
Firm: Tolleson
Art Directors: Steve Tolleson, Jamie Calderon
Designers: Jamie Calderon, Satomi Nagata
Production: Rene Rosso
Client: swissnex

Printer: PressArts
Method: Sheetfed Offset, UV
Papers: Cougar Cover 80 lb Smooth (cover),
Cougar Text 100 lb Smooth (text). Queen City
paper, Carbon (fly leaves)
Colors: 6/5 4 color + 1 PMS + AQ (outside
cover); 6/5 4 color with rich black + AQ (inside
cover); 6/6 4 color + 1 PMS + AQ (text); 5/5 4
color + AQ (pp 9–10)

Illustrators: Jamie Calderon, Satomi Nagata

Statement:

Swissnex acts as a catalyst and curator for new
ideas—sponsoring unexpected perspectives
and activities between the spheres of art,
science, education, and technology, functioning
as thought leaders in innovation and cross-
disciplinary exchange.

Swissnex magazine challenges the traditional
approach to annual reporting, expressing the
organization's activities and mission in a highly
visual way.

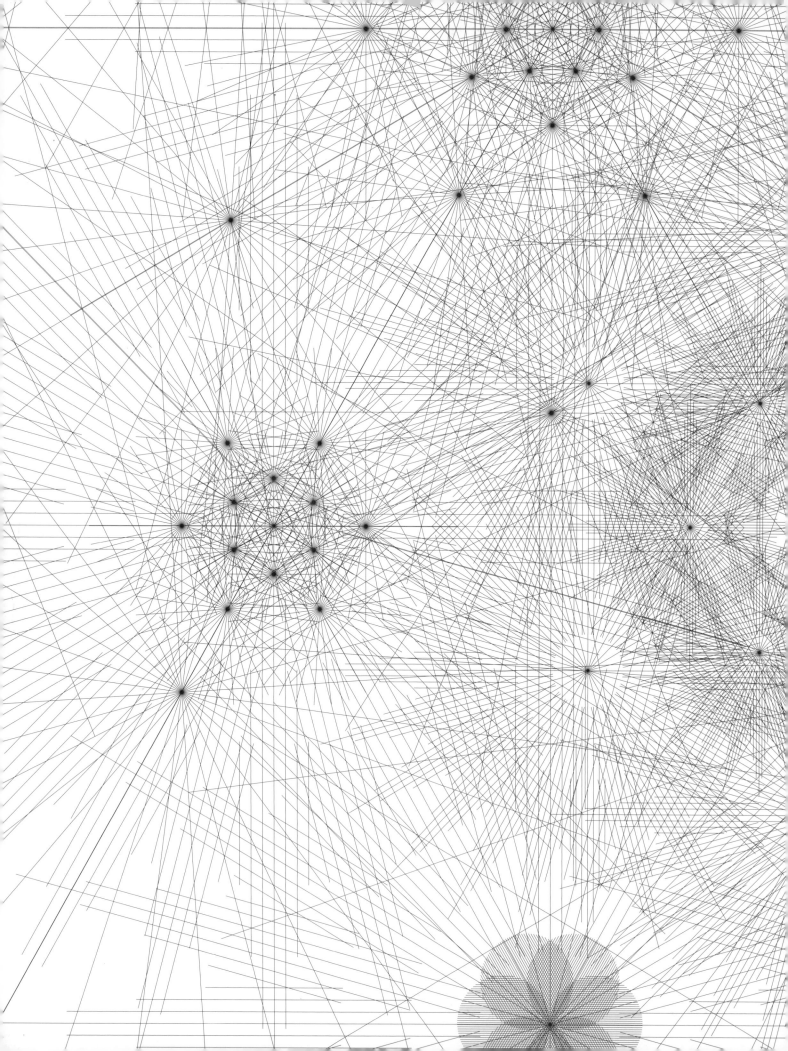